Partners in the Dance

Stories of Canadian Women in Ministry

Patricia Bays
editor

Anglican Book Centre
Toronto, Ontario

1993
Anglican Book Centre
600 Jarvis Street
Toronto, Ontario
Canada M4Y 2J6

Typesetting by Jay Tee Graphics Ltd.

Canadian Cataloguing in Publication Data

Main entry under title:
    Partners in the dance : stories of Canadian women
in ministry

ISBN 1-55126-072-7

1. Women clergy – Canada. 2. Anglican Church of
Canada – Clergy. I. Bays, Patricia.

BV676.P37 1993   262'.14371   C93-095431-9

Contents

*

Introduction

Some years ago, a group of Anglican clergywomen decided to collect the stories of Canadian women clergy as a way of sharing experience and telling the story of how the ordination of women came about in our church. All women ordained at that time, and some lay women, were invited to send in stories, vignettes, reminiscences, and many did. The project has taken a number of years to develop, but this book is the result of that collection. As the book progressed, some further stories were solicited to round out the collection and to represent other aspects of women's ministry in the Anglican Church of Canada. There are, of course, many women clergy whose stories are not told here. I hope that the process of telling our stories is one that will continue and grow. Through story we come to a new understanding of one another's experience. We share in the struggles and rejoice in the blessings.

I write this as we are celebrating the sixteenth anniversary of the ordination of women to the priesthood in the Anglican Church of Canada. To those women who have struggled for years to see this day, it seems like a long and painful development. Yet it is important to remind ourselves that we are still very much in the process of pioneering. Sixteen years is a short time in the history of the church, and the work of pioneering is lengthy. The stories in the early part of the book of women who trained for ministry in the 1950s and 1960s are a vivid reminder of how far we have come in understanding the ministry of both women and men. The acceptance of women as full participants in theological education and training has come relatively recently. The story of Lois Wilson, an ordained minister in the United Church of Canada, reminds us that, even where ordination has been permitted for fifty years, acceptance of women's ministry is still slow. As yet, there are few women clergy in senior positions in our church. But the appointment of Betty Garrett as Archdeacon in the diocese of Qu'Appelle, 1 January 1992, is a first to celebrate. While the period of pioneering may take a very long time, there is the excitement and challenge of being involved in something new, and there is much to celebrate in the faithful witness and dedicated ministry of women which we see recorded in these pages.

These stories show us the joys and tensions of women's ministry, and we are grateful to all the women who were willing to share their experience with the whole church. There is always a risk involved in story-telling. We reveal a good deal of ourselves, make ourselves vulnerable by sharing with others our deepest feelings and concerns. Clergy are sometimes put on a pedestal by others, are seen as authority figures, as different, perhaps as "better," "more spiritual." To express anger, doubt, uncertainty challenges these attitudes, takes the risk of revealing our humanity. We are glad that these women were willing to share their experience with us.

I have chosen as title, *Partners in the Dance*, which suggests to me a number of images. It suggests the partnership of women and men in the church, both in ordained ministry and generally in the life of the church. It suggests the partnership of clergy women and lay women, in which each should support the other in the struggle to define the place of women in the Anglican Church of Canada. It suggests the importance of networks for support and nurture and advocacy — networks of ordained women, of all church women, of women and men. Partnership includes other churches of the Anglican Communion, and we are grateful for the support of the Fellowship of the Maple Leaf in England for assisting with editorial costs. We hope that this book will be a vehicle for sharing our Canadian experience with others.

The dance is seldom solo or solitary. Others are involved as we move in the patterns and rhythms. Sometimes one partner leads, sometimes the other. Some independence is given up in entering into the structure of the dance; yet something important is gained. So, as part of a structured and ordered church, there are always tensions as we develop our partnership. But the dance is a celebration. It is a sign of life and hope, a movement which grows and changes all the partners in the dance. It is a symbol also of reconciliation. The movement may be gradual and tentative, with steps forwards and steps back. Yet the dance is in process, and this book is a celebration of what that means in the life of our church.

Patricia Bays

*

Issues around the Ordination of Women

The issue of the ordination of women is one that has been debated for many years and in many parts of the world. The ordination of women as deacons did not seem to generate the same emotion. The office of deaconess was an ancient one, referred to in the New Testament and developed in the early church. Deaconesses visited the poor and the sick, ministered particularly to women, and prepared women catechumens for baptism. In 1861, the deaconess order was revived in the Church of England when the bishop of London dedicated Elizabeth Ferrard to this work. Deaconesses were admitted to this order of ministry by prayer and episcopal laying on of hands. So, on the basis of a century of experience of this kind of ministry by women, the Lambeth Conference of 1968 accepted the principle that the diaconate be open to both men and women and that "those made deaconesses by laying on of hands with appropriate prayers be declared to be within the diaconate." Women thus were able to be ordained deacon with relatively little controversy, and many provinces still opposed to the ordination of women to the priesthood see no problem with women deacons.

But the ordination of women to the priesthood seems to have generated a great deal more controversy, and arguments have raged on both sides of the matter. What are some of the issues that have emerged in the discussion?

First among these is the question of how we understand and interpret Scripture. Women played an important role in the life and ministry of Jesus and in the early church. How do we define that role, and what do the various scriptural titles of office (elder, deacon) mean as they are applied to women and men? How do we interpret Paul's comments about the behaviour of women in church and their role in the developing Christian community? What does Paul's teaching about "headship" mean? In Christ there is neither male nor female. Yet 1 Corinthians 11 and 14 seem to suggest the subordination of women and a prohibition against women preaching and teaching. But women are clearly important figures in the life of the New Testament church and have had a valuable ministry of teaching and service down through the ages.

Second, how do we understand and interpret tradition? Prior to this century, the ordination of women has not been a part of church tradition. But tradition is not static. How does tradition develop and change? As we rediscover the legacy of many holy women of the mediaeval and later ages, how do we incorporate their writings and teachings into the received tradition of the church? How is what we are doing in the Anglican Church of Canada participating in the development of church tradition?

Third, how does our understanding of theology affect our practice? In theological terms, how are both women and men "in the image of God"? Is that image defined by maleness? Does God intend a different calling to women and men? Do exclusively masculine images of God reinforce this view? What images of God does Scripture give us? What is the essential nature of priesthood? How do priests "represent" Christ to the people? Is this through their masculinity or through their humanity? Do the personal characteristics of Jesus and his disciples determine the nature of priesthood? In what sense is priesthood related to the life and work of the first apostles? How do our attitudes towards sexuality determine our understanding of ministry? How are these attitudes changing and what difference does that make? As our society changes, what impact does that change have on the life and customs of the church?

There are practical areas of discussion. How are power and authority exercised in our church? Who makes decisions, and how do those decisions get implemented? How do women take their place in the structures of the church? What does ordination mean in the context of a renewed understanding of the ministry of the laity? How can we deal with the practical considerations raised by the ministry of women — part-time employment, job-sharing, maternity leaves, family life? Are these different for male clergy, or are we coming to a new understanding of the ministry and the daily life patterns of both men and women?

There are many books and articles and conference resolutions which have examined these questions in detail and from a variety of perspectives. The purpose of this book is not to argue the case. But these questions do form the background to the stories that unfold here and are questions which the church has been addressing and will continue to address. I hope that the women's stories will bring to these questions the perspective of their experience and will enrich the church's study of these issues.

Patricia Bays

*

History of the
Ordination of Women
in Canada

The issue of the ordination of women to the priesthood in the Anglican church is not a new one. In this century, as early as 1935, the archbishop of Canterbury had appointed a commission on the ministry of women which considered the matter, but, in its report, upheld the tradition of a male priesthood. In 1944, the bishop of Hong Kong ordained a woman, Florence Li Tim Oi, as priest, but there was such controversy over this action in other parts of the Anglican Communion that, following the war, she agreed in 1946 to cease functioning as a priest. Miss Li continued to study during the many years of upheaval for the church in China. When the churches reopened in 1979, she took up the exercise of her ministry again. In 1981, Miss Li came to Canada to visit family and decided to remain. In 1984, she was the honoured guest at a service in Westminster Abbey marking the fortieth anniversary of her ordination. She died in Toronto in February 1992.

The ordination issue kept reappearing and was discussed in many parts of the Anglican Communion. It was a topic on the agenda of the 1968 Lambeth Conference. The Section on Renewal in Ministry stated that it could find no conclusive theological reason for withholding ordination to the priesthood from women. The Lambeth Conference affirmed that the theological arguments for and against such ordination were inconclusive, and requested every province of the Communion to give careful study to the question and to share insights with each other. The conference recommended that, before any province made a final decision to ordain women, the advice of the Anglican Consultative Council be sought and considered.

At its first meeting in 1971, the ACC passed two resolutions relating to this matter.

We call on all Churches of the Anglican Communion to give their consideration to this subject as requested by LCR 35, and to express their views in time for consideration by the Anglican Consultative Council in 1973.

In reply to the request of the Council of Churches of South-East Asia, this council advises the Bishop of Hong Kong, acting with the approval of his Synod, and any other bishop of the Anglican Communion acting with the approval of his Province, that, if he decides to ordain women to the priesthood, his action will be acceptable to this Council; and that this Council will use its good offices to encourage all Provinces of the Anglican Communion to continue in communion with these dioceses.

Both motions were passed, the latter by a very small majority (24-22). On Advent Sunday, 1971, the bishop of Hong Kong ordained Joyce Bennett and Jane Hwang.

Also in 1971, the Canadian House of Bishops authorized the ordination of women as deacons. Those women holding the office of deaconess could become deacons. They were then recognized as being in Holy Orders.

In the interval between the 1971 and 1973 General Synods, the discussion continued in the General Synod Committee on Ministry and in the House of Bishops. At General Synod in 1973, after a long and careful debate, this motion was passed in all three orders:

That this General Synod accept the principle of the Ordination of Women to the Priesthood, that this decision be communicated to the Anglican Consultative Council, and that implementation not take place until the House of Bishops has worked out a pattern for the Canadian Church that would include an educational process for the Church.

When the ACC met in 1973, it noted that the bishop of Hong Kong had ordained two women as priests and that no Province had broken off communion with that diocese. A number of churches had begun serious discussion of the principle of the ordination of women to the priesthood. The Council recommended once again that, where any province decided to ordain women to the priesthood, this should not cause any break in communion in the Anglican family.

The Canadian House of Bishops met to work out a way to implement the decision of General Synod and presented for study by the whole

Church the process by which this should happen. At General Synod in June 1975, the following motions were passed. The vote is recorded in parentheses.

> That this General Synod reaffirm the principle of the ordination of women to the priesthood. (189–56)

> That this General Synod further affirm that it would be appropriate for women qualified for the priesthood to be ordained at the discretion of diocesan bishops acting within the normal procedures of their own jurisdictions and in consultation with the House of Bishops. (208–35)

> That no bishop, priest, deacon or lay person including postulants for ordination of the Anglican Church of Canada should be penalized in any manner nor suffer any canonical disabilities, nor be forced into positions which violate or coerce his or her conscience as a result of General Synod's action in affirming the principle of the ordination of women to the priesthood and requests those who have authority in this matter to act on the principle set out above.

In their meeting in October 1975, the House of Bishops agreed that the Communion be notified of the intention to implement these resolutions, and agreed that, if the responses of other Provinces were not overwhelmingly negative, bishops were free to proceed to the ordination of women to the priesthood after 1 November 1976. The first ordinations took place on 30 November 1976. The women ordained were Beverly Shanley and Mary Lucas (Niagara), Mary Mills (Huron), Patricia Reed (Cariboo), Elspeth Alley and Virginia Briant (New Westminster).

In the years that followed, there were a number of discussions about the continued use of the Conscience Clause once the period of transition was past. The National Executive Council affirmed in 1982 an interpretation of the Clause which affirmed its validity ''for those who belonged to the Anglican Church of Canada at the time it was passed.'' They went on to say,

> While continuing to recognize the rights of individual consciences, we believe that those who now come to membership or to any office or ministry in our church must recognize and accept that the ministry of women priests must also be protected conscientiously as the expressed will of our Church.

General Synod in 1986 rescinded the Conscience Clause and adopted the following statement:

1. this General Synod reaffirms its acceptance of ordination of women to the priesthood;
2. no action which questions the integrity of any priest or postulant on grounds of sex alone can be defended;
3. this General Synod honours all priests, upholds them in its prayers and desires that God's will be done in and through all priests, regardless of sex;
4. while Christian love cannot be legislated, it needs to be practised and demonstrated in the Body of Christ.

The movement in Canada for the ordination of women was not without pain and division. There were some who chose to leave the Anglican Church of Canada, and some who continued in the church have never been able to give approval to this departure from tradition. Yet, from the hindsight of sixteen years' experience of the ministry of ordained women, it seems to have been a relatively smooth and orderly transition, and women priests have taken their place in the life of the church alongside men clergy. The stories which follow reflect some of the struggles and pain of the movement towards ordination, but also the joys and satisfactions. They are city rectors, incumbents of multipoint rural parishes, regional deans, chaplains, members of diocesan and national committees, making a valued contribution to the life of the whole church.

Patricia Bays

*

The Early Days

In Canada, women began to study theology long before the ordination of women was even dreamed of. The early records of Trinity College in Toronto show, for example, that there were eight women students studying theology part-time in 1915. Throughout this century, women students formed a small but constant presence in this and other theological colleges, as well as at the deaconess training school, the Anglican Women's Training College. The 1956–58 calendar of Trinity College says,

> Women students properly qualified by university graduation are admitted to the Divinity course. They proceed to degrees in the usual way; however, they are exempted from certain courses in Pastoral Theology and take further elective courses in their place.

Postulancy for ordination was not regarded as a prerequisite for theological study.

The next four stories describe the experiences of some women who studied theology without any plans for ordination. Two — Thora Rowe and Phyllis Lock — subsequently were ordained. Two — Marjorie Powles and Patricia Bays — were not.

Marjorie Powles

My concept of ministry for both women and men is one of the ministry of the whole people of God. Moreover, Elizabeth Schussler Fiorenza's definition of the Christian community as a "community of equals" seems appropriate for defining Jesus' own ministry and the Church as the Body of Christ.

I grew up in the United Church of Canada, which began ordaining women in 1935. As I felt called to lay ministry, I attended Covenant College, which later became part of the Centre for Christian Studies, and took classes at Emmanuel College in company with the men and a small number of women who were preparing for ordination. My understanding was that we would all be working together in a variety of ways to serve the church as deaconesses, missionaries, Christian educators, or ordained ministers.

Following graduation I became General Secretary at McGill University of the Student Christian Movement (SCM) with which I had been associated as a student at the University of Manitoba. The SCM is an ecumenical movement and I found myself more and more attracted by the Anglican church. In Montreal I was confirmed as an Anglican, married a priest, and, together with Cyril, went to Japan, where we worked for over twenty years.

In Japan my choices were limited, and my profession became that of a teacher of English in both secular and church schools. In later years, in Vancouver and in Toronto, I taught adults in literary courses as well as English as a second language. I came to value the opportunity of the association with both teachers and students in a secular setting, and always experienced this work as ministry. At the same time, theology is my key to the meaning of life, and feminist theology has provided wonderful insights.

We returned to Canada to live in 1970. Here I was caught

up in the feminist movement in general and particularly in the Christian feminist movement. Although I myself have never felt a call to ordination as a priest, I have believed for many years that humanity is created in God's image, female and male, and that it is heretical for women to be barred from any role in the life of the church. Accordingly, I became active in supporting the movement for the ordination of women in the Anglican church, as well as participating in the struggle of women to achieve parity in all areas of church life. The struggle is far from over, but many in the church now recognize women's participation as a gift, not a threat.

Women for centuries have studied the Bible, taught children, studied and taught theology, been spiritual counsellors. We have not cared a lot about hierarchy and power, and I believe that this is our gift to the church.

Patricia Bays

Women have always been involved in the study of theology. They have reflected on the meaning of the faith, and have shared that knowledge in their conversations, in their writings, and in the classroom. I belong to the last generation of women who undertook the academic study of theology without any expectation of ordination. It seems to me one of the strengths of the Anglican Church of Canada in those days was that this formal study for a theological degree was possible for those who were not postulants for ordination. The church and the colleges were then, as now, open to the contributions of well-trained and theologically literate lay persons.

Although, in the early 1960s, some in positions of responsibility were undoubtedly thinking of the possibility of ordaining women to the priesthood, these thoughts did not impinge very much on the women studying at that time. I think that we embarked on our studies at Trinity College because of our interest in exploring the faith, our love of the church and — frankly — our enjoyment in studying! In my class, which graduated in 1965, there were three women students. One subsequently was ordained, and two of us were not. Women students traditionally led the class in academic achievement and were respected for those abilities. We were, however, not seen as preparing for priesthood and so were exempt from certain portions of the academic program. We did not attend the practical sessions on how to baptize or celebrate the eucharist, how to choose hymns or sing the service or plan for worship. In Homiletics, we could choose the option of preparing a series of Bible Studies rather than preaching in front of our classmates. Dr. Feilding did, however, make certain that we completed the full field work requirement, a kind of fore-runner of Supervised Pastoral Education.

As we progressed through third year, it was clear that the men students had a definite idea of the vocation for which their studies had prepared them. The women students, on the other hand, had to scramble to find some kind of appropriate employment. I worked as Director of Christian Education in a Winnipeg parish. The parish was welcoming and kind, but it was clear that there were few precedents for setting salaries, and for enabling the participation of professional lay workers in the life of the diocese. When visiting theologians were invited to speak to the diocesan clergy, what encouragement was given to theologically trained lay people to attend? Yet our training made that attendance an important part of our own continuing education.

Eleven years after our graduation, the first Canadian women were ordained to the priesthood in 1976. For myself, I made a decision to remain as a lay person, although I support wholeheartedly the movement for the ordination of women to all orders in the church. I do not feel a call to particular ministries in the church for which ordination to the diaconate or priesthood is necessary. My ministry is one of teaching and theological reflection, and of serving the church through its committee structures, and these are things that I can do as a lay person. In fact, I think it is very important that there be theologically trained lay people who are able to participate in the decision-making structures of the church and in the teaching of and reflection on the faith of the church. Yet I am sometimes conscious of the fact that I do not fit easily into either category. Trained with the clergy and having prepared people for parish ministry by teaching Pastoral Theology, I am not ordained and so cannot be a part of that group. I am a member of the laity, but my training and experience can set up a barrier that separates me from other lay people.

I think it is important that women take their place in all aspects of the church's life, including the ordained ministry. Every person has gifts which can be developed and used in the church. It is a great joy today to see the large numbers of ordained women, many now of long experience in ministry, using their abilities in the life of the Canadian church. Each brings her particular gifts and experience to enrich all of us. It is also a joy to see the number of well-trained lay women who are able to share in the ministry of the whole people of God.

To me, the importance of the contribution of women in ministry is that each woman is unique, a special individual with special skills and experience to bring to the life of the church. Where once half the population (and probably more than half of the active churchgoers) were denied the opportunity to use those gifts in particular ways, now we can acknowledge and celebrate those gifts, share them with each other, and use them for the glory of God.

Thora Wade Rowe

Prophetic eyes would have recognized indications as my childhood and youth unfolded that I might someday be a priest of the church; that is, if my gender had not automatically precluded the possibility. At least, so it seems to me in retrospect.

My father was a disabled former army officer, a veteran of the First World War: my mother the Irish V.A.D. who had nursed him when he was taken wounded to a London hospital. With a fierce tenacity we held to all things British, for we lived in the Quebec countryside, isolated socially from the English-speaking mainstream of society and culturally from our French-speaking neighbours.

Slowly and steadily there grew in me a longing for full-time service in the church. I cannot recall when I first recognized and identified my calling for what it was. Was the seed sown at my mother's knee as she would faithfully read my sister and me stories from the Bible as she put us to bed? Or was it on summer Sunday afternoons when I ventured to begin Evening Prayer in our little stone church, with never more that a dozen people present, on the occasions that the itinerant priest arrived late? Perhaps it was on summer evenings in my late teens when I would take the great iron key off its hook on our kitchen wall, walk through the woods behind our house, and open the church door to spend time playing hymns and repeating Evening Prayer by myself, only to be silenced by a sense of being suspended in time and space between the faithful of the preceding centuries and those who would follow after.

Certainly some seed was sown at diocesan church camp in my teens when I felt inexplicably stirred as an invited speaker, a theology professor, lectured us on God. There were also those wonderful teen years of discovery on so many fronts as I attended the English high school in the city nearby. But there was no greater discovery than dawned in confirmation classes, that the God "out there" was the same Jesus Christ "in here," loving me with a love I could not resist.

The seed was beginning to grow the summer of my early twenties which I spent vanning on the prairies with Sunday School by Post. With my companion I visited isolated Anglicans in their farm kitchens, conducted Vacation Bible Schools in the one-room schoolhouses of rural communities, and preached my first sermon to a small gathering of native people in the little wooden church on their reserve.

Thus, step by step my life unfolded. Acquiring an Arts degree led into teaching which I loved. There was only one thing that I realized I would rather do: study theology. That study meant enrolment at the Anglican Women's Training College in Toronto. I arrived to discover that having a degree gave me the rare, new privilege of enrolling in the full course in theology with men preparing for ordained ministry.

For three years I was the only woman in the full course at Wycliffe College. It was the mid-fifties. I belonged. I was at one with my brothers in spirit and vision in a way that seemed more significant than the ties with my sisters where I lived and received practical training. I even won the preaching prize one year! By osmosis I was preparing in mind and heart, to say nothing of skills, for the ordained ministry. The implications of this preparation seem to have been lost on everyone, not least myself.

Graduation and ordination arrived. Suddenly it was "they" and "I." When the majority of my classmates processed up the cathedral aisle for ordination, I found a seat in the side aisle through the kindness of a clergy widow who moved over to make room for me. A classmate was sensitive to my unanticipated distress, and invited me to share his family's celebrations, but this could not assuage my grief. "Well," as some subsequently commented, "what did you expect?" What indeed! I had failed to notice that I was not "one of the boys" after all.

At this time, a young priest, a special friend since my late teens, came into my life in a new way. He had just been made incumbent of a parish when we were married, and I started a new life that included being helpmeet, chatelaine of the rectory, eventually mother of our two children. In the service of induction to the two-point rural and village parish, the bishop wondered aloud, innocently, if the parishioners had realized that they were getting two for the price of one.

My husband had a compelling vision of all people being enabled to use their gifts regardless of race, sex, or status. It was bittersweet to work so closely with him, yet always as a volunteer and always within the structural prohibitions of the church. One year the parishioners elected me a lay delegate to Synod. This brought a wrathful telephone call from the bishop to my husband. "A clergyman's wife cannot be a delegate to Synod," he insisted. "It would be like giving the priest an extra vote." There was no satisfactory answer to my husband's questioning reply: "If my wife is neither clergy nor lay, sir, what then is she?"

It was not as though there were not plenty of opportunity to be involved in the life of the church. I taught the children in Sunday School. I co-led Sunday School teacher classes. As educational secretary, I taught the women of the Women's Auxiliary about the church's missionary work. I opened bazaars with a flair. I began and ran a Girls' Auxiliary. I visited parishioners. I took courses and attended workshops. The rectory door was always open and the table ready to feed whoever chanced by. Life was very full and I was using many of my professional skills. Yet the tension within me remained.

In my struggle to resolve that tension, I made a private pilgrimage to the place of my roots, only to find that the tree had been cut down where I had sat when I made an initial commitment to Christ at age sixteen. As well, the church had been sold because of the deaths or exodus of the few Anglicans, and in the front yard of this now-private residence, the baptismal font had become a planter. I recall saying to my husband when I arrived back home, "It is as though I have had a major operation, but I trust I will heal in time."

The local United churches were a light shining through my

struggle during those years, affirming my ministry by calling on me to take services for them from time to time. The clergy and people welcomed me warmly and gave me every encouragement. But somehow I could not leave my roots or settle for the sacrament of the Lord's Supper only occasionally. Yet sometimes in desperation I prayed, "Lord, if I can't be ordained, please remove the call." Seemingly, God was deaf. My visionary husband affirmed, "You will live to see the day when women will be ordained." But my husband was not to see that day with me. His sickness and death introduced years of a different kind of pain and struggle. I had found a way to serve in social work, and was to make a career in that field, but still it did not silence my call to ordained ministry.

Remarriage, this time to a layman, made life easier in some respects and more challenging in others as we worked at trying to construct a melded family with five diverse teenagers.

But a change in the mood of the times in the Anglican community began to impinge on my consciousness. I became aware that I was not alone in the world in my dilemma. Women began crossing my path — at first, amazingly, because they sought me out, increasingly because I sought them — women who spoke and demonstrated the raising of consciousness and its implications within the church.

Relieved of the financial burden of single parenting, I began working only part-time as a social worker and combined work with studies, commuting to the Toronto School of Theology. It was the United Nations' Year of Women! I was the first woman to earn a Master of Divinity degree from Wycliffe College. Pastoral Counselling courses followed at the Kingston Institute of Pastoral Care, and that experience helped me let go of my hurt and anger at the establishment. There was the encouragement of our primate's attitude and words, and the courage to approach a succession of authorities in the church about my sense of vocation. There was the inspiration that came from attending one of the first ordinations of women to the priesthood in the Canadian church. Throughout, there was a growing realization of sisterhood, and celebration of what I might have to offer as a woman, no longer aspiring to be "one of the boys."

Finally the goal was in sight, and I was afraid! The voices of all those who, over the years, had questioned and undermined my sense of calling, sounded in my ears. Besides, I was now in my mid-fifties, a time when most are planning for retirement, not a challenging new career. Yet affirming me was my husband, believing in me, planning an early retirement to support me. And then there were my now-grown children cheering me on: "Go for it, Mum!"

On 16 September 1986, in my ordination to the diaconate, I recognized my inner truth being confirmed outwardly. It was a day of joy beyond words. A number of friends told me of observing two rainbows in the sky as they were travelling to the service.

I divided my time among social work, home responsibilities, and a non-stipendiary role in my home parish, but there never seemed enough time and energy for the latter. In March 1987 I burned my bridges behind me and resigned my social work of twenty-one years' duration.

Priesting followed on 24 June 1987. What a joy that my first wedding was that of my daughter! My confidence grew as I assisted a knowledgeable, supportive priest. Only two parishioners refused to take communion at my hands. One was reconciled after a parish visit: the other chose to treat me as though I did not exist. You win some: you lose some.

In January 1988, the bishop appointed me as incumbent of a small, rural, two-point parish on a half-time basis. My joy is preaching and pastoring. My leadership is low-key: I function as an enabler, encourager, working for consensus. My parishioners are good, solid types, salt of the earth. A year after my appointment, I received confirmation of their support when they asked me to be full-time. The bishop in due course added his personal encouragement in making me a canon.

What does the ordained ministry feel like for me? It feels like arriving home, amongst loved ones, after a long trip. Praise God, it feels like being in the centre rather than periphery of God's will. The future? It seems enough to discover and work at the myriad implications of the privilege of ordained ministry.

After all, would it not seem to be superfluous to be personally ambitious beyond the achievement of a life-time goal?

In 1992, as I travelled to the centennial celebrations of the Anglican Women's Training College, its predecessors and successor, my whole life's pattern unfolded in poetry within me. I called the result:

A Personal Hymn of Praise to God for His Guidance and Blessings through the Years

"Thy Hand, O Lord, has guided Thy Church from age to age,"
And now, in my mature years, I turn another page.
Your blessings are unnumbered, on me, Your precious child:
Yes, through none of my virtue, the years on me have smiled.

God called me in the quiet of lonely, early years:
God called me to God's service despite my anxious fears.
Christ spoke to me, as Saviour: Christ challenged me, as Lord,
And, by His loving mercy, His Spirit on me poured.

I thank God for the people who taught and fashioned me.
I thank God for my sisters who helped to set me free.
I thank God for supporters — kind faces I recall —
For mother, husband, children: for Jesus most of all.

How can I praise my Saviour for gifts on me bestowed?
For parents, schools and friendships and more — my life is owed?
The clouds were sometimes heavy; the tears, with sobs, have
    flowed;
Yet You were there to guard me, and guide me on the road.

Joys broke o'er me like sunshine through my varied life:
As student, and as worker; as woman, and as wife;
As mother of dear children — I've watched them grow with
    pride —
And now, with years advancing, God's open'd His mercy wide.

The years ahead lie dormant: I cannot know their tale,
Yet each day calls me forward: I shall not fear to fail,

For God, Who led me thus far, goes with me on the way,
And I shall sing God's praises unto the endless day!

Phyllis Lock

C anada had fascinated me since I was a young child and, when
I heard the call to pastoral ministry, God did not keep me
in England but led me here. When I made inquiries about training here as a deaconess, I discovered that deaconesses were treated differently in Canada, and did not have the same kinds of
jobs as in England. It gradually became clear to me that I needed a theological education at a seminary in order to be acceptable in a diocese. Wycliffe College accepted me and the principal
said that I would be eligible for the same bursaries and grants
as the men. I, being naive, took that for granted. My classmates,
all male, were very careful not to say the wrong thing, and consequently spoke only occasionally; this restraint led to a very lonely
first year. I had to deal also with the conflict within me. By this
time I was certain that my call was to the priesthood but I also
knew that I would travel quite a distance to avoid attending a
church with a female priest. I had to come to terms with this.
During this time, I also met priests who preached one thing and
lived another. I discovered that the Anglican church was not the
loving, caring family that I had experienced up to this point.

During my studies, I gained a great deal of helpful pastoral
experience from parish placements and I shared in all aspects of
parish ministry. Prior to my last year, I served at St. Paul's Church
in Faust, Alberta. Again my naivete showed when I was asked
if there were Indians there; I said, "No, someone would have
told me." I arrived to find that this was a native community of
400 people, with only 6 white families. I was scared silly and spent
most of the summer carefully avoiding many people. By the end
of the summer, I realized that Indians were people and I became
comfortable with them. I expressed concern to my supervisor in-

dicating that if I had been more prepared I could have been of more use to the native people. His response was, "You were OK. They don't matter." I felt badly about this attitude and vowed that I would do all I could to counteract it in the future. Bishop Pierce wrote and offered me a place upon graduation. I was thrilled to have a job.

In September, the principal agreed to a bursary covering my tuition for the year, but, in January, he told me that I could not return as I had not paid my fees for the previous term. He denied this earlier conversation and said that the bishop of Athabasca had changed his mind about a job. Fortunately the office had a record of the bursary. In the end, I graduated with a reasonable grade in spite of the continued prejudice of two professors. This was counteracted by two of the other professors who supported and helped me.

In May 1972, I took a bank loan to enable me to graduate and travel west. During that last year I had been student assistant at St. Matthias, Etobicoke, and they held a "Going West" shower, giving me everything I needed — saucepans, dishes, sheets, towels. It was very encouraging. My mother had flown from England for graduation and she drove west with me. It was back to Faust. No surprises for me, I knew what to expect, but my mother was shocked by all the mud and near-naked toddlers wandering around day and night. The house had three rooms and was heated by a wood cook stove. My water was delivered by the barrel. I felt that the time I spent on survival activities was not what I had been trained for. After a few months I started to travel to McLennan for Sunday services — 75 miles in good weather, but over 100 if it was wet. Faust was a rough community. One night I had gas stolen from my car and it was used to start the fire that burned the store to the ground. We worked hard that night to contain the blaze. Most of the experiences were new, including attempted rape by a parishioner. I became an associate of the Sisters of St. John the Divine and found that prayer support a source of great strength. The bishop had me move to McLennan, into a house with running water, an indoor toilet, and a furnace. More comfortable, yes! Yet I found McLennan a lonely place as there was no great desire to keep the church open and to build up the congregation. The Roman Catholic bishop was very supportive and invited me to participate *fully* in their services. Throughout the years the Roman Catholic clergy have all been very supportive and helpful.

In March 1976, I went to Beaverlodge, a beautiful small town in a good farming district on the edge of the foothills of the Rockies. My almost seven years there were an enriching experience. The parish became involved in a Mutual Ministry experimental project. I was fortunate to see many people grow like buds coming into flower. The people asked the bishop when I could be priested. We had to wait for Provincial Synod, which passed the resolution in November 1976 in spite of the archbishop asking the synod not to. The bishop waited another three months until the fuss had died down. There were letters saying that we would split the church and were being instruments of the devil. I did not receive as much of this sort of mail as some women did.

On 7 March 1977, I was ordained priest in St. James' Cathedral, Peace River, with a man and another woman. All the doubts that I had not had before, came flooding in during that service. Was this of God or of the devil?? When hands were laid on me, it was as if the weight of the whole world was laid on me and I thought that I would collapse ... the weight ... the dark, ... the pressure.... When I was raised to my feet, it was like new birth, it was wonderful, triumphant, glorious.... I wanted to sing and to dance. The support of the diocese was wonderful then and has continued to be throughout the years.

While at Beaverlodge, I became a Civilian Chaplain for the Forces Station there and thoroughly enjoyed that experience. In 1982, I moved to High Prairie. The bishop said, "I need an experienced person who will go there and love the people and try to bring about some healing." The main roads had been paved by this time and travel was easier. The people challenged me constantly. It was a new experience for me to be challenged on everything I did. My first annual meeting there was a great surprise — people yelled and shouted at each other, thumped the table and walked out. I thought they would come to blows. As the years went by people grew and developed in their faith. We had a prayer group and the atmosphere in the church said that people cared.

A course on Life, Death and Transition with Dr. Elizabeth Kubler-Ross helped me to start to come to terms with many things in my own life. I continued to take her courses including the facilitator training. I learned to identify feelings and emotions and also how to express them. Though I say this, I was starting to experience stress at this time but did not realize it. In 1987 I moved to Slave Lake, an ecumenical parish where I served the Lutherans and United Church people as well as the Anglicans. The ecumenical movement is very important to me and I believe the Christian church needs to be seen to be worshiping and following the One true God. Slave Lake is a busy young community with a lot of transient people and few extended families. It was good to see so many young people in church and I greatly enjoyed being with them. I spent a great deal of time preparing people for marriage and then counselling as they tried so hard to stay together. Crisis counselling was also demanding and in the midst of this I experienced burn out.

I took sick leave but soon after my return to work I knew that I needed more time. I resigned the parish. After searching for help I found "Homes for Growth" an organization centred in the Winnipeg area where I could go for an extended directed retreat. Those four months were a life saver. I learned so much about myself and God, having time to integrate much learning that I had been too busy to assimilate over the years.

From time to time things happen to make me realize that not everyone accepts women priests. I was introduced to a bishop who turned his back on me. I find some of the pushy feminists very frustrating because they give more thought to their cause than to the church. Through this, the firm foundation was being chipped away. I could not identify exactly where and so was unable to do anything about it. Serving on the Diocesan Executive, the Bishop's Council, and being Rural Dean have helped to build my confidence and give me a great deal of experience. I was not always accepted, and every place had a few people who did not want a female priest. Many people have admitted their prejudice and said that it was not long before they felt quite different. Having a female priest was different and at times even better. I know that there were also times when a male priest would have been better and at such times I would indicate to the bishop that maybe it was time for me to be moving. In this way, male and female priests have been able to complement each other. The addition of women to the priesthood has enhanced the ordained ministry of the Anglican Church of Canada and has also helped people to have a more complete picture of God.

In 1988, I was thrilled to be made a canon of the diocese. It is one more opening that allows me to say how wonderful God is and to share what he continues to do in my life. I have made mistakes over the years and have therefore hurt others just as I have been hurt by the church. I have looked closely and questioned whether or not I wanted to be a part of this pain-causing institution. The pain-causing institution is only a part; for we are in reality the Body of Christ and Yes I want to be part of that Body. Acknowledging and feeling the pain enables me to say Yes to God when he asks me to be part of the redemption process which is happening in his church throughout the whole world.

*

Bishop's Messengers

A significant factor in the acceptance of women in the ordained ministry in Canada was the large number of women who had already been in ministry for many years. There were many theologically trained lay women working as deaconesses and parish workers in the north, in rural areas, in the inner cities, and overseas. Eva Hasell's Sunday School Caravan Mission sent "vanners" to rural areas to bring Christian Education to the scattered farms of western Canada.

One such group of women workers was the Bishop's Messengers, a lay order of women started in the diocese of Brandon in 1928. Marguerita Fowler was trained at St. Christopher's College in London, England, and commissioned by the bishop of Brandon to take services, to visit, and, in the absence of a priest, to baptize and to bury. She, along with Muriel Secretan, began work in Swan River, Manitoba. The Messengers were under the jurisdiction of the bishop and lived in St. Faith's House, a small house in Swan River with a chapel and a guest room. They took vows of obedience and regular prayer, but did not think of themselves as a religious order in the classical sense. Members wore a uniform and shared a regular pattern of prayer and meditation. Frances Wilmot was for many years Senior Messenger of the order. By the time of the dissolution of the order in 1979, there had been 56 licensed Messengers, all with theological training, but there were many other associates and helpers who shared in their work. The work centred on the Christian Education of children and on the establishing of parishes and the development of healthy and active parish life. Messengers built churches, travelled to distant missions often over impossible roads in hazardous conditions, preached, taught, gave first aid, worked with immigrant families and with native people. In 1958, St. Faith's House was moved to The Pas. Most of the work of the order was in the diocese of Brandon, with two exceptions — Eriksdale in the diocese of Rupert's Land and Pelly in the diocese of Qu'Appelle.

When the ordination of women became possible, a number of the Messengers were among the ordinands. These were women who had already been engaged in full-time pastoral ministry for many years, and they brought to their new role that wealth of experience.

Marjorie Kennon

I began my ministry in 1953 in the diocese of Brandon appointed by the bishop to a northern Indian mission on the "Bay Line" from The Pas to Churchill. I had just finished taking theology in Toronto and training for ministry. I worked as a Bishop's Messenger of St. Faith's, an order of women commissioned by the bishop to be in charge of isolated missions or rural parishes. We conducted Sunday services, took funerals, prepared children and adults for confirmation and baptism, did hospital and home visiting, led children's groups in the parish. A priest came in for the sacraments.

Cormorant on the "Bay Line" was an Indian settlement on the shores of beautiful, northern Cormorant Lake. The men went out on the trap-lines and fished for a living. One night the young men came into the mission saying that a pack of wolves had followed them home! There was no road into Cormorant, only the railway. Two Bishop's Messengers lived in the Mission House. We had a first aid station at the mission because we were the only medical help. We were surrounded by forest. The big event of the day was the train pulling into the station. The whole settlement went down to meet it. If a doctor was on board, the train would wait while he saw his patient before proceeding up the line. My first dog-sled ride was at Cormorant — thrilling! I taught at the school and helped at the Mission.

At the end of the year, I was posted to Moose Lake Indian Reserve, forty miles from The Pas. We went in by bush plane, sitting on the mail bags. As the plane came in for landing, we could see hundreds of children running, converging at the dock below. Small hands whisked every piece of luggage up to the school. We lived in the "teacherage" (part of the school), taught the children, and worked in the parish. There were three of us. There was no road or railroad in. We went in and out by bush plane or bombardier in winter with a load of fish, or by river boat in summer.

After two years at Moose Lake, I was posted by the bishop to the Swan River Valley where I worked under the direction of the rural dean, rector of Swan River. We ministered to seven churches in seven towns. I was there for nine years. It was old homesteading country — beautiful, wooded, rolling hills. In the winter, there were icy, snowy roads but the warmth of hospitality made up for winter cold and storms. The rector and I would meet at the early Holy Communion service at Swan River, then go our separate ways to take services at the other towns.

After nine years, I went to be in charge of two small towns, Kelwood and McCleary, and the surrounding farmland at the foot of Riding Mountain National Park. In the summer I did the religious instruction with children at the diocesan camp. I was ordained deacon in 1971 and was the first woman to minister to these parishes.

After eight years, I was called to serve the parishes of Carberry, Austin, and McGregor. It was a vast area, covering a thirty-five mile radius and included three other towns. I had three services on Sundays with thirty miles between them; I was again the first woman to minister there. I was ordained priest in 1977.

With ordination, I could finally fulfil my ministry. Before ordination, I felt cut off from entering fully into the life of the people in the great events of their lives — baptism, marriage. It meant so much to be able to give to the people the spiritual nourishment of the Body and Blood of Christ. Ordination to the diaconate and to the priesthood were occasions of tremendous joy and like entering the very ''courts of heaven.'' In the diocese of Brandon, we had no problems being accepted by the clergy because we had been working in charge of rural parishes for years.

At present, I am in charge of the parish of Coaldale, seven miles from Lethbridge, Alberta. During the war, Japanese who were interned in camps in Slocan City, B.C. were transferred here to work on the sugar beet farms. A Japanese mission was established here which became the present parish of Coaldale. The Japanese people, out of deep devotion, built the beautiful little church with volunteer labour. Today there are still some older Japanese and two young Japanese families in our congregation, but otherwise it is occidental. I still bring communion to some very old Japanese in Lethbridge and Raymond. I was the first woman priest in the diocese of Calgary.

*

Women Priests Tell Their Story

The stories which follow represent a wide variety of experience in ministry. Some women have found ready acceptance of their ministry. For others, such acceptance has been more difficult. Women serve in all sorts of places and in all sorts of ways — rural and urban parishes, chaplaincies, teaching. The breadth of their experience is reflected in these stories.

Muriel Adey

I am Co-ordinator of Pastoral Care at a 450-bed general hospital, paid by the Anglican church, and am priest incumbent of the nearby, small, parish church. Without doubt, these have been the best years of my life.

I grew up in northern England, was confirmed at the age of fourteen, and was active in the church youth club until I left for university. The curate who nurtured the youth club let me browse in his library and initiated many debates about the implication of the faith and its applications to everyday life. He was exacting about attendance at communion and kept us on our toes. Had I been a boy, I would have been a server and it would probably have been taken for granted that I would "enter the church." I was not a boy.

Four years at university, a degree in biology, and a teaching diploma saw me teaching high school students. I deliberately taught evolution in such a way as not to make it seem incompatible with Christian faith. I married — which was not originally in my plan! Soon we had three children, and the privilege and responsibility of bringing them up. As opportunity arose, I worked part time at a variety of jobs and also continued to read widely in theology and philosophy. I was very frustrated with clergy who, when asked to recommend books to read, could think no farther than devotional ones, all of which I had read earlier in my teens before tackling meatier stuff.

Eventually my husband's career gave us the opportunity of coming to Canada in 1967. To my utter amazement, people were talking about the time when women would become ordained. I did not know what to think! I just couldn't imagine hearing a woman's voice saying the service, never mind a woman's hands offering the Blessed Sacrament. Yet. . .! I sat on the fence until after the first women were ordained. People would ask me why I wasn't one of them. My answer was that, had it been possible when I was twenty, then I would have offered myself, but, now that I was forty-six, I rejoiced for the young women who could devote their whole lives to ordained ministry.

One Sunday in 1976, the sermon put me on the spot. It was about people who put themselves into boxes, limiting themselves. I went back into church that afternoon and prayed that I would be shown whether God wanted me to attempt the road to ordination. One way God could show me would be to open doors. I could not see how we could afford for me to go to seminary. Our children were thirteen, sixteen, and nineteen, the expensive ages! That very evening, my husband returned home from a six-week research project to say, out of the blue, that he had been wondering whether there was anything that I would like to do, now that the children were growing up. I gulped! I took a deep breath — and told him I would like to go to seminary! In 1981, I graduated with the M.Div. degree but lived in a diocese which had not even begun to consider ordaining a woman. I was invited to train in pastoral counselling at a local centre and I discovered an aptitude, so I undertook formal training through the Canadian Association for Pastoral Education (CAPE). In 1987, I qualified as a Specialist in Institutional Ministry. Meanwhile my diocese had a new bishop, and ordination as deacon and priest took place during CAPE training. After I had served for one year as university chaplain and associate priest in a parish, the chaplain of a local hospital retired and I stepped into his shoes at the hospital and the parish. In 1990 the hospital began to contribute some money to the diocesan ''pool'' set aside for chaplaincies. The parish has always paid for its share of my time.

I am still full of wonder over the way God fulfilled my deepest dreams, even though I submitted my own will to that of my husband and his plans. I smile sometimes as I recall those people, mainly men, who were so bitterly opposed to the ordination of women. I continued to travel to and from seminary even when it appeared that there was no prospect of ordination, because I would not give them the satisfaction of thinking that a woman could not make it! I am even grateful that ordination did not follow immediately on completion of seminary, for the delay gave me opportunity to discover a completely new field — chaplaincy. The very fact that I became the only CAPE-qualified priest in the diocese gave me entry, not only to the hospital where there was a vacancy, but also to the parish which shared the chaplain. I learned not to let people limit themselves to the known and the safe but to dare to risk and trust. After all, our God continues to do new things as a matter of course and we are bidden to look forward, not back. It could not have been done without the encouragement of my husband, sons, and daughter. I feel that they are saints — they had the work at home while I had the exhilaration of studying what I had always wanted to study.

Elspeth Alley

It was on the eve of my confirmation that the thought of the priesthood as a vocation entered my head. I was twelve years old and had just completed three years of weekly lessons that were required before I could be presented to the bishop for the laying-on of hands. At the close of my last class my parish priest asked me to kneel in front of him so he could offer a prayer for me. He kissed the top of my curly head, gave me a blessing, and in that moment I felt the presence of God in that place. I got up from my knees, walked out of the room and thought, "If I were a man I'd be a priest." I had never before felt God's presence as strongly as I had that afternoon and for a short time my thoughts were consumed with the desire to serve God as a priest to his people. But I had to face the cold hard fact — the priesthood was open only to men! Forty years later when the bishop laid his hands on my head I remembered my thoughts as a twelve-year-old and I said out loud, "I am a woman and now I am a priest."

My journey toward ordination (although I didn't know it then) began when I entered the Anglican Theological College in the autumn of 1965 as a part-time student. My youngest daughter had been attending Sunday School classes in our parish church and every week she came home with the same account of Moses and the bulrushes. I enrolled in the college because I wanted to learn about our Anglican tradition and to understand the Gospels as they relate to our lives today. There, with enough knowledge, I would teach teachers and they in turn would teach the children attending Church School.

I was accepted as a part-time student knowing that I was to take the same courses required of the theological students who

were working toward ordination. I was prepared for the difficulties of returning to school as a mature student, but I wasn't prepared for the hostility within those academic walls. When I arrived
the first day of classes, with my black academic gown over my
arm, I walked down a long hallway and listened to my footsteps
resounding on the stone floor. From the other end of the hall
a short, stocky man, a second-year student I learned later, walked
toward me and when he came near enough he said, "I just want
you to know that for every moment you are in this institution
I will make your life as miserable for you as I possibly can." And
he proceeded to do so. No one, faculty or student, knew what
to do with a woman in an institution where students were planning a vocation in an all-male field. I was told that there was
no need to update and validate Sunday School teaching and I
was asked why I wasn't at home baking cookies for my family.
I was more or less on my own except for one or two students who
befriended me. I was not allowed to eat in the dining-room or
even to pass through with a tray. I ate my lunch in my car or
in the recreation room below. Offensive remarks about women
were made by some students and one member of the faculty.

A few days after I arrived for classes, it was suggested that
perhaps I would like to spend my study time in a small room
at the end of the hall. The librarian would get my books, I was
told, so there was no need for me to go into the library. I replied
that I wouldn't know, until I looked in the stacks, exactly which
books I would need and I expressed concern over not being able
to interact with other students. My comments were ignored and
I was led to the door of the library. We stopped, and the professor remarked on the names, printed on the door, of the benefac-
tors. I said, pointing to the name at the top, "She is my
godmother and I don't think she'd be too pleased if she knew
that I was not encouraged to use all the library facilities." Any
suggestion that I was to use the room at the end of the hall was
never spoken again.

My husband and my children were very supportive and wanted
me to enjoy my new endeavours. I came home many times in
tears and, after I had written my Christmas exams and passed

them, I decided to leave. I was angry with the church and angry with "those" men but every day, after I had left the college, I knew I had to go back. I fought with God for two years — "Get someone else," I said — but he won out and I returned to the college in January of 1968.

The situation at the college had changed. The new student body was composed of men who had worked in the secular world and had later responded to God's call to the church. They agreed that Sunday Schools needed good teachers and the curriculum needed to be updated. I was not allowed to eat in the dining-room but students sometimes brought bag lunches so we could be together over the noon hour. The faculty were supportive and encouraging and the students were both friendly and helpful.

The turning point in my life came one day when a reporter from one of the daily newspapers called to ask if she could interview me because "it was so odd for a woman to attend a theological school." I sought the principal's approval and asked him if I should avoid the question of the ordination of women to the diaconate which was, at the time, being discussed as a proposal in the House of Bishops. He misunderstood my question and said, "But you want to teach — you aren't interested in ordination, are you?" And I found myself saying, "It's not for me to say what I'm to do — it's for God to say." The principal said, "Go and see your bishop — he will give you direction."

The Anglican Theological College and Union College amalgamated in 1971 and became the Vancouver School of Theology. When the principal was installed, the student body processed in academic robes, and friends of both colleges attended the ceremony in a downtown church. When the service was over I was pulled out of the procession and lifted off the floor by a recent graduate of A.T.C. and a newly ordained priest in a neighbouring diocese. He stared into my eyes and said, "I understand you are seeking the diaconate. If I ever hear that you are seeking the priesthood, I'll kill you." That night my arm was so badly swollen that I had trouble getting it out of the sleeve of my dress, red marks appeared under the skin where his fingers had pressed so savagely.

Archbishop Somerville ordered me deacon on Pentecost in May 1972. I served in St. Catherine, North Vancouver, until my husband died in 1974 and I returned to the city. I assisted a priest in a small parish near my home and in June 1975 I was a curate in a large parish. On St. Andrew's Day 1976 I was ordained to the priesthood. In January 1977 my bishop appointed me priest-in-charge of a small Christian community in Richmond and in 1979 I was inducted as rector of a city church of about one hundred people. The congregation was elderly and because it was an apartment area there were few children.

In 1985 I resigned to write a biography of Archbishop Scott, primate of the Anglican Church of Canada. The book was published in 1992 in time for the meeting of General Synod in Toronto in June.

I have been very happy in my ministry. I have had two supportive bishops and, for the most part, supportive members of the clergy. Except for a few, members of congregations have been responsive to a woman priest and, to those who have not, I have learned that it is their problem, not mine.

I have had many opportunities to serve beyond my parish boundaries. I have served on Diocesan Council, on Advisory Committee on Postulants for Ordination, on the Senate of the Vancouver School of Theology, as Senate representative on the Board of Governors. I was elected for two terms of office as a delegate to General Synod and had the privilege of celebrating the eucharist on the banks of the Trent Canal in Peterborough one Sunday morning in June 1980.

My time at the Theological College was not easy and I was definitely a pioneer. I never fought to be ordained. I believed that if it was God's will it would occur, and it did. Today, in 1992, I serve as honorary assistant at St. Philip's Church, Vancouver and from time to time I "fill in" as Sunday Supply to churches waiting for their new incumbent or for priests wanting a vacation. I am now of retirement age but I still work as often as I can and go wherever and whenever I'm invited to help in a parish. The ministry to the people of God is my vocation. I love my work and want to continue as long as I am able to do so.

Alyson Barnett-Cowan

W hen I first went to theological college in the fall of 1972, I had no intention of becoming a priest. The question simply didn't cross my mind, since it hadn't occurred to too many people yet, at least in those parts of the church which I had inhabited, that women might be priests. My divinity career began as an intellectual quest: I wanted to study theology because I wanted straight answers to questions that had arisen from my reading and earlier studies.

These were not, I admit, questions that everyone spends time over. I wanted to know, in simple English, what words like *ontology, homoousios, hermeneutics*, and *homiletics* meant. I wanted to understand biblical commentaries that would suddenly zap in a Greek word, in Greek letters, so that I couldn't even pronounce it. And, above all, I wanted to have a solid understanding, for my own faith, of what the church teaches about God, us, the purpose of the universe, salvation: the whole package. I thought at the time that the only place to find out these things was in a theological college, even though I had a feeling that there was something wrong with having to take an M.Div. degree to get straight answers.

It hadn't occured to me, until I went to college, (in arts, at the same school) that I was a second-class being. My parents had raised me as a thinking, feeling person worthy of respect, and I grew up thinking that the subordination of women was all in the past, not a factor in my generation, or even my mother's (she worked full-time, and had been an officer in the war). It was divinity students who taught me otherwise. I discovered that there were some (I must stress, just some) men, preparing to be priests, who truly believed themselves to be superior intellectually and emotionally because they were male.

There had been women in divinity before — women who had been very esteemed by these men. But, I was told, they had made sensible choices — they had either become nuns or married priests. It was made very clear that if I had a vocation it must be to one of these two states of being.

In my heart I knew that these choices were not the answer for me, and I wanted to prove them wrong — but I had been intimidated. I was really scared when I approached the dean to ask if it was possible to apply for admission to divinity. I stressed that I just wanted to do the academic part — I didn't need to do field work, since I wasn't going to be ordained. He proved not to be such a frightening, august being as I had convinced myself he was, and he very sensibly persuaded me to take the whole M.Div. program and leave my options open.

My classmates in divinity immediately began to tell me how I couldn't — mustn't — shouldn't be ordained. "I don't *want* to be ordained!" I kept saying. "Good," they said, "because you can't."

After a while, I began to question this assumption. Just as I had believed that I had a brain and could read theology, I began to realize that perhaps there was no particular reason women should not be ordained, even if it was inconvenient. (In my last year in arts, the battle was fought, and won, to have women servers in chapel, and the greatest problem seemed to be that it made the servers' parties integrated.) I began to reflect on the nature of the tradition of the church, about what was essential in it, and whether and how parts of it could change in new realities without violating the truth of God. I was convinced that the Spirit of God was at work to preserve what needed to be preserved, but also to bring new life and to give voice to new expressions of God's truth.

I didn't have to articulate any reasons for the ordination of women until 1974, when I was asked to take part in a debate on the subject with Cyril Powles, against Wayne Lynch, a fellow-student, and Eugene Fairweather. It was frightening to go "up against" the angelic doctor, but he made the whole task easier by not arguing very persuasively. We found out later that he'd already been convinced in favour! Cyril and I won the debate, and it received a lot of coverage at the time, but I still had to deal with my own feelings.

I'm a person who likes to work through structures, and I had been upset with the American "valid but irregular" ordination in Philadelphia. As an ecumenist, I took seriously the potential threat to possible reconciliation with Rome if we went ahead unilaterally. I had a number of friends who were wrestling with whether they could stay in a church which betrayed, as they thought of it, Catholic teaching. I didn't like the "it's my right to be ordained" approach of some women, since I saw it as a matter of divine call rather than human rights. I went to the first ordination of women in Niagara in 1976 in some emotional turmoil; looking back, I think I had internalized the anxieties of my male friends, and somehow thought that the roof might cave in! In one sense, I suppose it did: the Church *has* changed since that day.

I myself had been ordained deacon in 1975, but the bishop who ordained me retired, and his successor couldn't find any work for me. I stayed on at Trinity as Eugene's theology tutor, and had the opportunity of working with women coming into the school truly with all their options open. I had been the only woman in my class — except for one other who was so disgusted with her treatment by our classmates that she switched to the United church at Christmas. In the first class I tutored there were three, and by the end of my time there were many women of all ages, who had secretly wrestled with vocation to the priesthood and had kept hearing what I had heard — "You can't!" They began to study, full or part-time, and the faculty was never the same again. They brought the perspective of people who had lived in the world for some time before studying, people who had lots of experience of the church from the pews, people who wanted to talk openly about sexuality and gender in the church. They were exciting students to teach, and they asked questions that went far beyond the intellectual curiosity I had started with.

I didn't marry a priest. I married a deacon, and we were

ordained priest together in 1978. Our experience of trying to find
employment together in the church makes an interesting story
— once we spent a nerve-wracking half-hour with three bishops,
one at a time, as each of them explained why they wanted one
of us but not both. In the end, it was one of those series of coin-
cidences which faith recognizes as grace that led us to Schefferville in northern Quebec, where Bruce was rector of a parish and
I taught theology in another form: religious education for adoles-
cent Naskapi Indians and Newfoundlanders. We both began to
learn theology again from having to translate what we had learned
via the European tradition into two other quite distinct cultures.

Our experience there led us to our later work, teaching
Swampy Cree Indians preparing for lay and ordained ministries.
(For some reason, Henry Budd College has more female students
than male. This is unusual for programs for Aboriginal leadership in the church, and we think it may have something to do
with the example of the Bishop's Messengers in this area.)

I have certainly learned, in Schefferville and The Pas, what
hermeneutics means! One task of theology in both places is, very
clearly, to translate stories. The biblical story of wandering peoples, of peoples honouring the land, of peoples in search of healing
and wholeness, comes alive in a new way with people who pitched
their tents in the frozen sub-Arctic, who relate in a spiritual way
with God's creatures, and who have been brutally mistreated by
their conquerors.

Women here have to struggle with many issues. The rate of
abuse is staggering — eighty per cent of women are sexually
abused by the age of eighteen. Sexual issues are not normally
discussed in public, and it is difficult to challenge male domi-
nance in leadership. Men, too, have suffered abuse — many children were raised in the residential schools, which, if they were
not outrighly physically or sexually abusive (and some were), were
certainly destructive of family structures. Children grew up without
any models of how to parent, and so have awkward relationships
with their parents and their children. Some marriages were
arranged by parents when the couple were teenagers; learning
about the theology of marriage based on free consent can be

troubling. Building self-esteem is probably the most important task of theology in this area — but perhaps that's not much different anywhere.

I still love reading theology. I haven't lost my romance for patristics (even though I have a hard time forgiving Augustine for the way he treated his mistress). But theology is not just an intellectual exercise. It is about empowerment for the marginalized, about strengthening the weak, and building confidence before God, about healing and the grace to change and grow. The invitation into God is for all of us, for ordinary people in all of our cultures. It should never be kept as the secret wisdom of a privileged few, who have to meet certain cultural expectations to be admitted to the inner circle.

Helena-Rose Houldcroft

It still surprises me that a person from the beautiful, rugged countryside of Central Ontario should end up on the Prairie flats of Saskatchewan. When I first began studying theology at Trinity College, Toronto, I never imagined myself living and ministering in the West. I, like the other women in my year, had difficulty finding a diocese that would offer ordination. It was at that time possible for dioceses to opt for the "conscience clause" and refuse to ordain women. My home diocese did not ordain women, so I had to seek support elsewhere. As an "unknown" approaching another diocese, I was placed low on their priority list. None of the women in my year were ordained when all the men were. I nearly decided to return to nursing but I accepted a position as a lay chaplain at a university. I had the deep pleasure of affirming my gifts to do ministry, and discovered the "authority" that comes from just doing authentic ministry and the freedom to make daring mistakes without a watchful diocesan eye!

During my two years as a chaplain, I was in conversation with Michael Peers, then bishop of Qu'Appelle. I had had little response from him and assumed that he was just one more uninterested bishop. But I persisted and, to my surprise, he chose to take a chance and ordain an unknown. On 14 February 1982, I was ordained deacon in the University Baptist Chapel, surrounded by many ecumenical friends and colleagues.

Michael was anxious about my acceptance in the diocese. I would be the first "import," and the first younger woman going into a rural, multi-point parish. I was oblivious to all the difficulties that might be ahead and saw only wonderful possibilities. Michael arranged for me to fly to Saskatchewan to meet with the parish. It was late fall, barren and snowy, and hardly any trees — just flat! There was an emergency in the parish that necessitated my doing a service on my own. A sermon was hastily written in a half-hour drive and I had my "baptism by fire." Having looked each other over, it was agreed that I would go to Big Country parish as an assistant. It was the middle of January when I loaded up my small car and left Toronto for southern Saskatchewan. I left behind my family and close friends to venture to a place where I knew no one. The trip took three and a half days of long winter driving to arrive finally in Saskatchewan. Thus began my ministry in a nine-church parish, spread over seven thousand square miles. I celebrated my priesting with them on a snowy St. Mark's Day in April.

As an assistant, I served only a short time before my name appeared on the list for a parish seeking an incumbent. I was surprised to learn that my name was at the top of the list. After such a short time in the diocese, I was treated with great respect. I have come to value the style of ministry in the West. In Ontario, I experienced the road to ordination as fraught with political overtones. I am a fairly direct and upfront person and was not always adept at political manoeuvres. I was also deeply aware that there was much you had to "earn" as clergy and that those who were junior had their place. I know others who relate very well to that dynamic. However, in the West, I appreciate a more personal approach to the ordination of women. People work out their opinions and concerns in relationship. There is opposition to women's ordination here but I do not experience it as politically entrenched. I believe that I am respected for what I have to offer in leadership and vision. I was appointed rural dean after only three years as a priest and have held a variety of positions on committees within the diocese. In our diocese, whether you are junior or senior clergy, there is a sense that you can run freely with a vision. Our diocese is not without conflict, but there is a general respect for honesty and openness. The issue of women's ordination has exposed the broader issue of our roles and sexuality as men and women. I think that awareness will bring a brighter perspective as the experience of women in orders grows. I hope we are gaining a realization that ordaining women is not a "women's issue" but rather a challenge to the community of believers to be whole and inclusive.

There have been many firsts for the diocese and myself. I was the first priest needing maternity leave and, after some consternation, we have in the diocese a very sensitive Parental Leave policy. I am the sole wage-earner in our family and it is my spouse who has chosen to remain at home. After serving in two rural parishes, I was appointed to a small urban parish in Regina to help provide leadership in some innovative approaches to outreach in a new area of the city. I went to the interview seven months pregnant with our first child. I discovered that my talents in leadership were much more an issue than my pregnancy! I am now expecting our second child and am enjoying an energetic and demanding ministry.

I have all the qualms and insecurities of anyone trying to do good ministry. I am fortunate to enjoy considerable affirmation and support. There is opposition and at times I feel it keenly, but nothing can remove the fact that I am doing ministry. It feels like a tremendous gift and privilege. I also know that it is a privilege as a priest to have a flexible schedule. I am able to nurse my babies and have a deep commitment to my family, at no cost to parish ministry. There are however unpredictable hours and evenings away that have my spouse wishing I was in any other vocation. I have never felt that any tensions surrounding the ordination of women were my problem. I carry on the best I can to emulate an authentic ministry. I am sensitive to the tensions in others but have always tried to meet that with openness and healthy communication. We still have a long way to go in understanding ourselves more fully as men and women. There are many women's stories that need to emerge if the community of God's people is to achieve wholeness. I am confident that, if we allow an atmosphere for women to do ministry, the experience alone will bring much healing.

Linda Nicholls

My story is not one of rejection or pain or struggle but of affirmation, support, and encouragement. I write it in the hope that it will be a sign of encouragement to others that the church can change and open doors for all people who are called to serve God through ordination.

My name is Linda Nicholls and I am a parish priest in the diocese of Toronto. My journey to the ordained ministry has been an outgrowth of my desire to serve God wherever I might be called. That call had originally taken me, as a teacher, to serve for five years in India. Upon my returning home my desire for theological education led me into parish field work as part of my studies. In that placement and with the encouragement of my rector I began to explore a change in vocation and consider the ordained ministry. Throughout the months of applying to an Anglican seminary and to the diocese as a postulant, I was conscious not of the unusual aspect of being a woman seeking ordination, but of seeking to hear God's voice and the voice of the church through those considering my applications. If the doors opened and my call was affirmed, then well and good. If they had closed, then I was prepared to serve in another capacity. The doors did open and I had the affirmation of the various interviewers, the diocese, and seminary entrance.

I completed my seminary training in 1985 and was placed in a curacy in a large suburban church within a senior citizens' complex. My time there was challenging, fulfilling, and supportive. I was challenged by the demands of team ministry, working with an associate priest and the rector. I discovered some of the strengths that I, as a woman, could bring to pastoral ministry, particularly with other women. Yet I renewed my conviction that ministry is not defined by our gender but by who we are as individuals and the gifts we bring to ministry.

After almost two years I was invited to be the incumbent of a one-and-a-half point parish on Lake Simcoe. Although women incumbents were relatively new, I had the privilege of following a woman incumbent in this parish. It was somewhat to my surprise that I was selected, as I expected the parish to choose a male successor. My selection was a tribute to the ministry of the previous incumbent and an affirmation that gender is not so strong a deciding factor as we may want to believe. By succeeding a woman the task of breaking ground in expectations and acceptance had been accomplished and I was able to move readily into ministering as pastor and priest without the heartache and rejection that some have experienced. Rather, I had to face my individual weaknesses in ministry, not because I am a woman but because I am "me."

I served for four years in that parish and was then invited to become the rector of a large, multi-staff parish north of Toronto. Here I am the first woman incumbent and successor to several long incumbencies. My reception here has been positive for the most part and, as in the past, the doors open most easily through pastoral ministry as I share in crises in the lives of parishioners. The greatest challenge has been to accommodate my leadership style to the rigorous demands of a large institution with multiple staff and to recognize the depth of the change in image and authority that my presence, as a woman, brings to the parish.

In all of my ministry I am keenly aware of the necessity of an external support network that can help me to keep my perspective, challenge me, and care for me in the midst of high stress. This is particularly so as I am single. The nurturing of family relationships and friends is critical to my personal identity which at times can be swallowed up in the demands of pastoral and priestly expectations.

Occasionally I am asked to express my greatest frustrations or joys in ministry, with the underlying assumption that these must be related to being a woman in ministry. My experience has been that my greatest frustrations and joys arise out of the same situations my male colleagues find — the struggles with old buildings, the strain of financial worries, the joy of pastoral intimacy, the exhilaration of preaching, the privilege of touching peoples' lives with the love of God. My greatest encouragement is in discipling — in watching people blossom as they are put in touch with God and with themselves and continue to grow.

I pray that others may also find affirmation and encouragement as they seek to answer God's call to serve in the church, male or female. May our gender be less important than the gifts we bring to share in the community of God's people!

Karen Binding

G od has played a dirty trick on me. I have been led on a journey of discovery, a journey that has distanced me from the
very church that nurtured me most of my life. I was baptized
a Christian in the Anglican church when only a few weeks old.
My parents' families had always been Anglican and we attended
church regularly when I was a child. I joined the junior choir when
I was seven or eight so I could stay in church to worship. I didn't
want to be downstairs with the babies! Our organist and choir-
master in Moncton was an energetic and warm man who worked
hard to make us a full part of the choir. This made me feel a
valued and appreciated member of the community. He believed
in us!

When we moved to Winnipeg, I joined the choir and encountered clergy who valued my opinions and taught me to think
for myself. The church supported me through nurse's training,
preparation for marriage, life as a new mother after a time of
infertility, and nine years of work as an intensive care nurse. Clergy
involved me in committees and believed in my abilities to chair
committees and organize outreach projects. They supported and
encouraged me when I finally voiced my sense of vocation to the
priesthood, a vocation that I had felt from the age of ten. I was
surprised that no one laughed at me. I was taken very seriously!

My desire to study theology was the catalyst provoking a full-
blown crisis in my husband's life and thus in our marriage and
family life (we have three children). We went through a rough
year as I explored the possibilities and he reassessed his priorities
and values. We emerged, thanks to the support of our parish
community, with a deeper, richer marriage. Life would never be
dull, and never be the same again! During our crisis, I discovered

how important my vocation was and that I would have to stand on my own two feet if I were to continue on this path. For three years or more Bob was not convinced that seminary would not pull us apart. He supported *me* but was not sure that all this was a good idea! Yet I always felt the presence of Christ. Through fear, anxiety, anger, passion, I was convinced Christ was calling me to share his healing presence with others.

I finished my degree and began looking for a job. Suddenly my direction in life was not so clear. I spent more than four years "filling in," priest-in-charge, then assistant. It seemed as though my church was not listening to the same Holy Spirit that I was. I encountered discrimination everywhere. Jobs opened up, but parishes wouldn't consider a woman or the bishop decided, "It would be better for you and your family to stay in the city." It was a very painful time. I felt betrayed by the very church that had encouraged and fed me all along.

In May 1985, I decided to take a course called Women and Theology, organized by a small group of women and led by Dawn McCance. We explored, discussed, and analyzed many books of feminist theology. It was an exciting and unnerving course. I made many discoveries about myself and about my opinions and theology that fit. I was indeed a feminist and a post-modern thinker. I believe that there is no ultimate authority but that we all begin from our own experience, share our truths with others, listen to their truths, and grow to deeper and broader understanding of what is true for me or for you. I came a little closer to wholeness. While I was taking the course, I was being interviewed for two parishes for the position of rector. It was a confusing time. As I let go of much traditional theology, and the security I had enjoyed along with it, I was being interviewed for jobs as the tradition-bearer. I knew that I had gifts and talents that would be good for the parishes but I wondered if I would be true to my new discoveries, my new sense of who I was, if I accepted either of the positions. I was appointed rector of the parish of St. Mark, the first woman in our diocese appointed rector of a city parish.

If faithfulness means continuing even when a person has no

feeling of the presence of God, no sense of peace or security, then I have been very faithful. I continued, week by week, to preach, to preside at the eucharist, to administer, to visit, to counsel, to love the people, often feeling a fraud. My first glimmer of hope came during Advent when I realized that I could preach with integrity again when the focus was on God's call for justice. I had experienced much injustice, even though I am a privileged, middle-class, white woman. I saw others' suffering and I knew, if there was a God, s/he would not want that suffering for anyone. A few month's later, I began to realize that I still felt connected to the eucharist and to the people. Women know what it is to shed blood, to give life. Women know what it is to pour out their lives for others. Women know what it is to share their bodies to nurture others. "This is my body given to you. This is my blood shed for you." Even the triumphal, hierarchical language of the eucharistic prayers could not sever me from my connectedness to Christ and the people.

Although there are many things in the church's traditions and theology that I do not agree with, that I do not believe, I don't know of any other place where I hear the call for justice and compassion. The church is unjust but the world is unjust as well. The patriarchal, hierarchical church must change or we won't be able to bring healing to the world. We are the ones in society who must be calling for justice for all.

God has played a dirty trick on me: nurturing me, loving me, and betraying me in the same church — calling for a deeper, stronger commitment to healing the world, removing all my props and supports, making me change, compelling me to call for change in my church so we *can* bring healing to our world. Most days I wouldn't want it any other way.

Barbara Minard

My story begins a long time ago. I was born in 1925 when the world was very different from today. I've seen many changes, and I find change exciting. Perhaps that is because Jesus brought change into my life, and through the years Jesus has continued to change me.

I cannot remember a time when God was not a part of my life. As a youngster I was very shy and afraid, but I trusted God to take care of me. I remember when I was around five or six my mother used to send me to our dark, spooky, mud-floored basement to get potatoes for dinner. Each time I did this, I was scared, but never told my mother because I was afraid she would think I was being silly. I prayed all the way down the stairs and up again, and when I reached the top safely I said a prayer of thanks. This was the faith of a young child.

I was a PK (preacher's kid) and found this a very difficult stigma in school. I was looked on as a "goody-goody," and felt I was different from the others. When I left home to attend Acadia University I wanted to forget I was a PK, I wanted nothing to do with anything religious, but God had other things in mind. In my third year of university, through the Student Christian Movement, God took hold of me in a very special way. I realized I was somebody because God cared about me, and God began to help me overcome my feelings of inferiority. In return for what God had done for me, I wanted to do something for God, and how I wished I had been born a man so I could become ordained! But this was impossible in the 1940s. As second best, I told God I would become a missionary. After graduation from Acadia, and two years of teaching, I was accepted at the Anglican Training College. However, this was my will, not God's, and God intervened. Because of a sudden change in life at home, I was not to train for missionary work. For the next three years I taught school, then married Bob.

During the next many years, almost thirty in fact, I forgot about wanting to be a missionary. I married, had four children, and moved ten times because Bob was a banker. Wherever we lived I became very involved in the church, teaching Sunday School, working for the ACW, on the Church Council, and as a lay reader. A variety of parishes gave me different church experiences, which I look on now as God's way of giving me a broad outlook on what goes on in congregations. I also did my part in many community activities, especially in the Girl Guides, and all this experience was excellent training for what I am doing now. I struggled many times with what St. Paul meant by being in the world, but not of the world. I found how difficult it can be to put God first in everything, and later these struggles would give me an understanding of what the average woman in a con- gregation is going through. I struggled, my faith grew, I lost my shyness, I loved people, I had a wonderful family. Life was good!

In the fall of 1980 I attended a conference sponsored by the Women's Unit of the Anglican church. It was during this con- ference I heard God calling me to ordination. This was the first time I had met ordained women, and throughout those four days my head was swimming. I didn't hear much of the conference. I only heard God saying I could be ordained, and I kept saying such a thing was impossible. I kept thinking, "If only I were youn- ger!" The Lord kept calling, and I kept up an inner argument with God for two years before my rector discovered what was on my mind. His response to my argument was, "Age has nothing to do with ordination." Next I told my husband and found him very supportive and encouraging. It was as if God had already prepared Bob for what was ahead. I waited till our youngest fin- ished school, and in 1984, at age fifty-eight, I began my studies for a Master of Divinity and ordination. During the first two months of lectures my head pounded from all I was trying to absorb, but since I am of Scottish ancestry, I told myself I would have to stay till Christmas because I had paid for the first term.

Miraculously, the headaches disappeared at the end of two months and I was able to continue. Bob was very supportive during those three college years, even though we saw each other only on weekends. He is still my greatest fan and listening ear.

On 1 May 1987, I began my work in the parish of Port Hill, Prince Edward Island. I had graduated from the Atlantic School of Theology two weeks earlier, and now Bishop Peters had sent me to this delightful rural parish, with warm, thoughtful people, and a magnificent rectory. I was thrilled! I was not to become deacon until September, but this parish had been without an incumbent for eight months. I was welcomed with open arms.

Ordained ministry was to become everything I had ever dreamed it could be. I began by visiting the sick and elderly — and there were lots! In less than four months I had eight funerals — an excellent way to become acquainted in a parish! I was ordained priest on 12 June 1988. I did what every parish priest does — worship services, visiting, Bible study, sermons, and too many meetings. I never felt a rejection from my parishioners because I am a woman, but a few rejected me because they didn't agree with changes I made. In spite of these few, new life began to spring up in the parish. Through the continual guidance of the Holy Spirit, I knew that our Lord was in charge. I just had to follow his leading.

There are things I found discouraging in parish work: 1) Congregations could be so much larger, if only people would realize the difference the Living Christ can make in their lives, but people seem to be afraid of the word commitment. 2) There are those who do not want to see any changes, and will fight against anything that is done differently from when they were a child, yet Christianity is about change. Why can't they understand this? 3) People criticize, and sometimes what they say reaches my ears. At times like this I have to remind myself they are not my boss — God is! 4) Sometimes I am told I must keep on the good side of those who support the church financially, but I let this go in one ear and out the other, and do not treat those with money any differently from the ones on welfare — in fact I visit the latter more.

I am learning patience. I like to see changes in people, because God wants all of us to grow more like his Son, and I would like to see these changes happen quickly (I think this is the greatest reward a parish priest has!). But God keeps reminding me that these things will happen in his time and in his way. I am only his instrument. During my years of parish work, I have learned a lot about caring and love because I have been shown so much caring and love by others. I fail many times, yet our amazing God continues to use me. This is the most satisfying work I have ever had.

Gladys Spurll

When I entered seminary, I was fifty-seven years old, in the process of divorce after nearly twenty-five years of marriage, and had three teenagers still at home. It seemed to many that I had set myself an impossible task, but my bishop insisted that it could be done. Although I was apprehensive, it seemed a wonderful thing to be able to study, for three years, the subject I was most interested in — theology.

I had no idea what the training would involve or how far I would be stretched but, apart from the stress of not knowing the outcome, I enjoyed every minute (or almost every minute) of my training. I especially enjoyed the collegiality of those with whom I studied. We formed a community which gave me a lot of moral support at a time when I sorely needed it. It was most unexpected. I had not known how I, an older woman and in such circumstances, would be received. I need not have worried. My children were not overjoyed because we lived in modest circumstances for these three years but we managed. Friends helped. We did not lack for anything we really needed.

I was ordered deacon in October 1980. That was the most thrilling moment of my life. There were three of us made deacons that day at my own parish church, and the place was packed solid. All my friends and all my children were there.

My first six months, I worked with Indians from the Fairford Reserve who were living in Winnipeg. That was a most useful experience for me, since I am English and had had no previous experience with native people. I felt a bit like a social worker. We were loaned a small chapel in a church. After services, we had coffee and bannock. Then one day my bishop asked me to go to a church whose rector had just had a heart attack. I stayed with that suburban congregation until they had a new rector. During that time, I was ordained priest.

As my time there drew to an end, I was approached by a man with whom I had trained to assist him with six country parishes in south-western Manitoba. My youngest daughter was graduating from high school and I was free to move. I had always loved the country and looked forward to a few years away from the city. I spent four years there, two as assistant and two as rector. When I was sixty-five, the bishop gave me a ten-months' extension. I left these parishes and returned to Winnipeg just before my sixty-sixth birthday. I was very sorry to leave, having mastered the art of juggling six parishes and driving countless miles in all kinds of weather. I was placed as priest-in-charge of three parishes near the city for a year and was really too busy to miss Pembina Hills at first.

Now I am honorary assistant at a church in Winnipeg and for a time was on call at a large hospital to bring sacramental care. This seems to be as much as is good for me to do, although I miss being in charge. I appreciate more time off. I am thankful for good health and hope that there are many years left that I can help out where I am needed.

Recently I had a holiday in England and met several groups of people who belong to the Movement for the Ordination of Women. They were interested in knowing my experiences and that those experiences have been positive. I hope they found it encouraging.

Cheryl Kristolaitis

W hat does it mean to exercise an ordained ministry? How does one give direction to the gifts and abilities which God has given and the church has affirmed and use them in such a way that the community of Christ is strengthened? For me, the exercise of this ministry has been in a variety of settings — as a curate in a parish, as a chaplain in an Anglican school, and as a program consultant for children and youth in a diocesan office. Each has had its own particular joys and challenges, yet in all of them I have been particularly concerned with communication, inclusivity, integrity, and the development of the ministry of the baptized.

One of my primary concerns has been communication, and, specifically, how to speak about the gospel of Christ and the beliefs of the Christian community with a clarity that does not result from over-simplification. This issue is as important in a parish setting as it is when working with children and youth.

Designing highly participatory educational programs which communicate clearly and openly has been part of all my ministry experience. To me, one sign that communication is happening is when a participant of any age joins the "conversation" by offering his or her insights. An example of this is a discussion of the Holy Spirit I had with Grade 5 children. As part of the program they wrote poems or paragraphs about how they understood God's Spirit to act. One girl read her delightful poem to the class. In it she compared all the loving acts of her mother to support, comfort, guide, and encourage her to the activity of the Holy Spirit in our lives. Mutual communication of the "good news" was occurring.

To enable mutual communication in a diocesan office is more

problematic. It takes time and both written and personal communication before people in parishes believe that program staff
really *are* willing to travel to them and work to meet their program needs. Even more important is the development of networks, so that people can learn from and support one another.
But with sustained effort it does happen. Days when the telephone rings again and again with requests for resources or ''long-
distance problem solving'' are signs that it is working.

Another continuing issue of my ministry has been inclusivity. Inclusivity is a matter of language, attitude, and structure.
For the community of Christ to include women and men, the
young and the old, it is necessary for the language we use to
include them. If I preach at an all-age service of worship and my
sermon does not speak to all ages in the examples I use or the
points I make, it is excluding some members of the community.
If my language is exclusively feminine in its imagery (a fault seldom found in our church!) then it is exclusive language. The language of the Christian community is true when it invites people
of great variety to enter with equal value.

Being Chaplain at The Bishop Strachan School was a great
help in my learning this truth. The school is made up of students who are Christian, Jewish, Hindu, Buddhist, Muslim, and
of no faith background. To include *everyone* in worship meant
honouring the various faith traditions present, while still
acknowledging that, from a Christian perspective, any graciousness of spirit I experienced was the graciousness of the Christ.
The Christ who wanted all of them to grow spiritually, without
coercion, but with respect for themselves and one another.

If the language is welcoming, but the attitude and structures
are not, little is gained. I truly believe that children and youth,
by virtue of their baptisms, are called to minister in the community. They can both give and receive pastoral care, pursue justice
and peace, learn, and teach. This requires that we change our
attitude and structures to enable them to do so. For example,
putting on an intergenerational, diocesan outreach workshop that
focused on Korea, South Africa, and Brazil, with a planning team
of people ranging in age from eight to over sixty, meant chang-

ing the style and times of meetings, as well as designing a program that was creative, concrete, and active. The day was evaluated highly by participants, but for me the real learning was in working inclusively to develop an event that was inclusive in language, attitude, and structure.

A third concern of my ministry is that of "equipping the saints." The ministry of the baptized is the foundation of the Christian community. Enabling baptized persons of all ages to identify and practice their individual ministries is a large part of my ordained ministry. Whether it is starting a student Amnesty International group, training servers, leading a workshop on storytelling, or identifying pastoral care issues with church school teachers, I see what I am doing as strengthening people in their identity as ministering people. Providing opportunities in parishes, deaneries, and the diocese for people with common ministries to gather reminds us all that we share this ministry.

And if the foundational ministry is the ministry of the baptized, then worship is most enlivening when it reflects that. One of the joys of my ministry has been working with children, youth, and adults as they develop the liturgy. Baking bread, writing the prayers of the people, proclaiming the word, creating the vestments, writing the collect and prayer over the gifts — all are ways in which the liturgy has reflected the particular community who gather to worship.

Recently in our diocese we have developed holy day events for All Saints' Day, Ash Wednesday, and Ascension Day which combine education and worship. Tears come to my eyes when I see a young child at such an event bringing something he or she has created to the altar as part of the offertory, or hear the prayers of the people reflect the language and concerns of all who have gathered. It is not always neat in its format, but it is always revelatory.

Lastly, my continual struggle, like that of all in the Christian community, is to live with integrity. That means working with the institutional church on key issues that affect its life. Being part of a task force in this diocese that has worked to develop a diocesan sexual abuse policy and follow-up education has been very rewarding. It is as important (and as difficult) to live with institutional integrity as it is to do so personally.

My personal "integrity" issue has been living out what I believe about valuing children with my three young children. Trying to ensure that I do not overwork and exploring the dynamics of my compulsion to do so has been a continual and evolving process. It has been my spiritual struggle. I have worked full-time and part-time, and, most recently, job-shared my position. Each change I made was with the purpose of living a life that balances personal and corporate responsibilities. Caring for the church without caring for myself or my family is a distortion of the gospel. I have always known that theoretically, but working it out pragmatically has been a source of learning and growth.

We have now moved as a family from Toronto to North Bay, where I continue to explore, in a new setting, the themes that have characterized my ministry thus far. I am co-ordinating an education project for the AIDS Committee of North Bay and area, and a pastoral team for the parish of Holy Trinity, Temiscaming (Quebec). At the same time I am the honorary assistant at St. Brice's, North Bay and do contract writing and training. We never journey alone or without purpose.

Phyllis Keeper

When I took Chaplaincy Training I went to classes, attended conferences and workshops, and also did Bible studies. I was assigned a few hours of time in hospital wards. I had many experiences during that time.

On one ward, a woman was brought in from up North. She was about fifty-three years old and could understand only very simple words in English. Her first language was Saulteaux. When she realized I could speak her language, she was really happy and asked me to visit her whenever I had time. I really got attached to her. I visited with her every chance I had. She asked me what my job was in the hospital. She didn't understand the word *chaplain*. I don't think there is a word to say chaplain in my language. I wasn't ordained so couldn't say I was a *minister*. I told her I was training to learn how to work with people in the hospital and to pray with them if a patient or family requested. She was so happy to find someone to pray with her.

She started telling me about herself. She was in a very weak condition. She had lost a lot of weight. She told me that her daughter-in-law had died with cancer and left three little children. They were three, four, and seven years old. One of the interpreters had interpreted for her that morning. She understood that she had to have a very serious operation. She started talking about her grandchildren. She said, "I wouldn't worry so much if I didn't have those three little kids."

She had to stay in hospital for a while because she had to build up her strength. She was quite weak when she arrived in hospital. When she went into the operation, she was still unconscious two days later. I went to see her doctor to have him tell me about her. He knew I was always there for her when I had time. He told me, "She is very, very sick. She waited too long to see a doctor — and has been suffering quite a while. If she had come in as soon as she knew there was trouble, it would have been better." I explained to him that you can't always do this on a reserve.

The third day after her operation, I had to leave. As part of my training, I had to write a paper about Genesis, do a presentation, and attend a conference. I didn't want to leave her. I talked to one of the supervisors of my training and was told I would fail in this part of the training if I didn't attend the conference. I was worried about her. I kept on praying with her when she was unconscious. I remember the last time I went up to see her, I really prayed and held her hand as I prayed. She never moved.

As I prayed, I told her, "I have to leave. I have to go because of my training. I will be back in ten days." I prayed that I could let go and I prayed to God that her grandchildren needed her so bad here on earth, but whatever is God's will. I felt as though she was my own sister. I wished always to treat the patients as my own family. I thought of how I would feel if the patient was my own sister, my own daughter, or my own mother. I prayed "Whatever happens, God, take care of it." I prayed that the children would be in a home where they would be loved if something happened to their grandmother. I knew that I didn't have the power to do any of these things. I had to put my trust in God. When I went into the conference, there was a chapel there. I prayed there. My prayers showed me that I was trying to do things myself. I was trying to be there for her — instead of letting God be there for her. Sometimes we are in God's way when we can't let go. I felt so much better when I felt that I could let go and let God work with her.

When I came back ten days later, I was still sometimes not believing. Sometimes we lose the feeling that God is going to take care of things. I avoided going to see her when I came back. I went first to the wards I was assigned to. The last ward I went to was her ward. We were very busy, and when I came back, I didn't trust enough. I was kind of afraid to visit her. I was afraid I would find out that she was gone. I thought the nurse might come and say she had died. That's why I went to visit her last.

When I went into her ward, she was sitting there swinging her legs over the side of the bed and eating lunch. And she said to me, "Oh, Phyllis, I'm so glad to see you back. I thought they might send me home before you came back. You know, I knew that you'd been praying for me." I told her about how I felt, how I was so scared. God shows us how many things he can do — and yet we still don't believe. We were hugging and crying together. When I saw her before I went away, she had many machines attached to her body. When I came back, she was only on intravenous. She was doing well and told me she was going to be going home that week sometime.

She said, "Let's give thanks to God. See, I can eat my meals too." She took her bread and wanted to give me half. I told her "No, I won't have half because that is all you have — and you need it to build up your strength. But, I will take a small piece and we will share it like the eucharist and give thanks to God. If I had been able to give eucharist like an ordained priest, I would have — but I couldn't. So, I took a cup of water from the sink in the ward and we had eucharist with water and bread.

It hurts me often not to be able to give eucharist, especially to Native people. They really need it. In their minds they just feel so much better after eucharist. When people have been ill and everything seemed almost without hope, and then they are healed — this is the time to celebrate! In those times, I so want to be able to give the eucharist.

When I go to the eucharist, I go to the cross and remember how much he suffered for my sins. I picture him talking to his disciples. I know he gave them bread — but he gave them more. He gave them his spirit. This is what he does for us. His spirit is invisible, but it comes into us.

Then, I praise God. Many people suffer from guilt. We don't forget about our wrongs. We learn from them. We ask God to give us his love when we hurt other people.

We are his instruments. He put us here to help others — those who are not strong, and those who don't know him. When I prepare people for the eucharist, I tell them my own experience.

I explain that Christ died for them. I also look to see what I might learn from them.

We also have to learn when to let go and let God do his work. We have to have enough faith to not try to do it all ourselves. That is what I did when I was with the woman at the hospital. I thought I had to be there all the time. I learned from this that I have to let go and let God and not be in his way.

Christina Guest

My story is not glamorous, nor even particularly exciting, but it shows that God acts in very ordinary lives, using very ordinary people, to spread an extraordinary message. I was born into a Christian home and was thoroughly acquainted with the ways of the Anglican church, its liturgy and its ethos, but I did not meet the Lord in a way that made any difference until I left the church.

The most formative event in my life, the one which more than any other contributed to who I became and where God fitted in my life, occurred when I was fourteen. My family was involved in a road accident which left my sister dead and my parents both physically and emotionally injured. My other two siblings and I walked away with a few bruises but many internal scars. Our family was torn apart in the years that followed. None of us seemed to have the inner strength to help one another find healing. We were so wrapped up in our own pain. My response was to retreat to my inner world and build up protection against the world. I left the church for most of my adolescence. The God proclaimed where we worshipped held no answer to the questions I was facing. I led a very angry and lonely life. I studied in Switzerland for two years and, on my return to Canada, enrolled at Laval University. It took less than a month for me to fall apart, since I could not cope with feeling so alone in the midst of the crowds on campus.

God had not abandoned me when I abandoned him. I attended a prayer meeting and watched a group of people pray to their God with the kind of joy I craved. What they had, I desperately wanted. The next day, a Christian friend invited me to a Bible study in her room and, after inviting me to ask God to make himself known, I felt all the carefully erected walls I had built come crashing down. This was a significant turning-point in my story.

Life had to begin afresh. I began to study theology at St. Paul's University, Ottawa. If I was going to believe in this God, I would have to know about him. Believing should make a difference. At this time, studying theology was a purely intellectual exercise. I undertook it assuming that God would show me what to do with my life. While my mind was being fed at St. Paul's, my spirituality was being nurtured at St. George's, an off-beat parish in downtown Ottawa which attracted those who felt that they didn't fit into "normal" parishes. It was shepherded by a man who had a tremendous ability to preach and live the marvellous redemptive love of God, a God who could take misfits like us and make us into disciples. The first proof that his message contained the power of God for me came when I fell in love with another "misfit." Our priest told us that he thought the Lord was crazy in calling us together, but God's hand was clearly working in us and we prepared to be married. Three months before the wedding, and in the third year of my studies, I experienced a call to ordination during a lecture on the presence of Christ in the eucharist. As the professor spoke, God said, "Make me present." Although I had not followed any of the procedures regarding postulancy, the church at the parish and diocesan level was able to affirm my call. My fiancé also affirmed that we would live out this call as each new stage in the journey became apparent.

I was ordained deacon in May 1986, priest in December, and served two years in the suburban parish of St. Stephen's, Ottawa. I began ordained life knowing I had much to learn, including the role of the priest in this day and age. In 1988, I became the priest in Russell, a small town half an hour from Ottawa. Ministry in a small town took on a different pace and flavour from city life. More happened in a visit to the Post Office than I could consciously schedule. Just being available led to some powerful encounters and moments of healing.

In 1990, our first son was born. His arrival stretched my understanding of my calling, and the need to balance professional and personal priorities became acutely felt. I have learned more about the love of God and the lengths to which it calls us to give of ourselves as a parent than in any other experience. Parenting has provided a rich harvest of sermon illustrations. In 1992, we mvoed to a new parish, six weeks after the birth of our second son.

The two boys could not be more different, and neither could the two parishes. Moving to Quebec, I became a member of a minority overnight; and the shock of that has made me see the challenge facing our church today in North America — learning how to live as a minority, along the lines of the ''remnant people'' theology we find in Scripture.

Ordination has offered me the privilege of being invited into very profound, meaningful, human and spiritual situations. I gain as much as those to whom I minister from our encounters. The priestly role of offering to be a sacrament of Christian servanthood to the church and the world has been rewarding. My pastoral theology has evolved out of my experience of the accident and more recently of parenting, as well as from the insight and sharing of those whose lives have touched mine. I am acutely aware of being used as a channel through which God has chosen to work. I am thankful that I was able to hear when God called; making him present is a never-ending challenge.

Edna Perry

I was ordained 24 March 1981, in the diocese of Rupert's Land and continued my secular job as principal of a large elementary school until 30 June 1983. At that time I retired after thirty-five years working as a teacher, education consultant, and principal. When first ordained, I served as an honorary assistant along with two full-time priests in a five-point parish. After a time as honorary assistant in a large city church, I was asked to serve at St. Cyprian's Church, Teulon, Manitoba. This is a rural parish, located forty-five miles north of my home. I commute each Sunday, make parish visits, and conduct services at the four senior citizen homes. I am non-stipendiary and receive a car allowance and a gift for each service.

For various reasons, including the shift of rural people to the urban areas, the church fell upon hard times in the 1960s and 1970s. Twelve women kept its doors open. It was then served by a priest as part of a three-point parish. The need for a more permanent presence in the parish led to my being posted there. The congregation is mainly retired people, with about five young families. However, there are now twenty-three children registered in Sunday School. There is a very active Junior ACW group and a Senior group, who do a great deal of fundraising to build a new Christian centre attached to the church. The people of Teulon are warm and friendly, and are striving to live their lives as committed Christians.

It frustrates me that my parish and home are so far apart. This curtails my participation in many parish events such as evening Bible study and young people's gatherings. At my age, I am not a keen night driver on Manitoba winter highways! The regular winter conditions of fog, ice, drifting snow, and blizzards have caused me at times to turn back. I am fortunate in having a very capable lay reader in Teulon; she takes Morning Prayer in my absence.

* * *

I have become legally blind. It happened Christmas Eve 1989 after I had taken a 7:30 p.m. service in Teulon. I drove home the forty-five miles and have not been able to read print or drive since. However, I have just about completed learning braille at CNIB.

I am fortunate in being placed as an honorary assistant at St. Catherines', Birds Hill. I am priviledged to take services — I memorized the service — I am still a padre to Royal Canadian Legion #7 and chaplain to the Rupert's Land Diocesan Mothers' Union. I have also preached at St. Simon's, Oakville, Ontario and in Devon, England.

Kathleen Bowman

As a Christian, I am first called to ministry, and within that I am called to ordained ministry, and within that I am called to parish ministry. As a student I felt that call very strongly. Now, with much more confidence in my abilities in ministry, I still feel that call. My experience of ministry has been very rewarding for me, but it certainly has not always been comfortable.

I was ordained deacon in May 1984 and priest in March 1985. At the time of ordination I was placed as a curate in a large urban parish, where I remained for almost seven years, gradually taking on more and more responsibility. I found the first couple of years quite difficult. The transition from college to parish is rarely easy, and like all newly ordained clergy I made mistakes. I believe that my mistakes were remembered longer than those of my male colleagues. It is easier for both clergy and laity to forgive the first bad sermons of a newly ordained man than those of a newly ordained woman. I found that I had to live up to high expectations with very little meaningful feedback or support. Fortunately I survived, and I started to enjoy the parish. I enjoyed building up relationships in the parish, and I found a great deal of satisfaction in pastoral care, preaching, liturgy, and teaching. I believe that because I am a woman I present and represent a spirituality that is different from that of my male colleagues, and that was appreciated by the congregation.

As I responded to people's needs and interests in the parish, my inner rage at the place of women in the church diminished. I did not have the energy to maintain it, and I became part of the community in a conservative parish. I learned that there was very little interest in the parish in social justice issues or in feminism. I learned how to be silent at the exclusive language and I lost something of the radical edge of feminism. I still struggle to keep in touch with the social justice community and I respond to any interest in these issues in the parish, but I am cautious about initiating programs and projects. I am no longer radical, but I have survived. It is a trade-off which I regret, but which I could not avoid.

I have made a conscious effort to be non-threatening to my colleagues and to parishioners, but I hope that I am not seen to be too passive. I have attempted to find a leadership style that allows me to express my views clearly and listen openly to others. I find that women clergy are perceived to be too powerful and therefore threatening, or too weak to survive in a parish. It is very difficult to be strong, but non-threatening — and that is what women clergy must do to survive.

My marriage in 1987 to an active parishioner was the best thing that could have happened, in terms of being accepted in the parish. I was now seen as "normal" in this suburban parish, and I now had more personal support, which reduced the normal stress of ministry considerably. The people of the parish were delighted by our marriage and by the birth of our first child, both signs of new life, and both giving me new status. I am very distressed by what this says about the status of single clergy in parishes.

My first position ended after a new rector was hired, and I was home for a time, waiting for the birth of my second child. Since then I have done part-time, interim ministry. It has been good experience to be in different parishes, and good experience to be priest-in-charge of those parishes. Working part-time has allowed me to spend more time with my young children. However, there is a certain insecurity, because I never know when or where the next interim job will be. I have not been able to find a permanent parish, partly because I am not mobile for family reasons, but also because women are not often hired. At present, there are no women rectors in this diocese, and that angers me.

I do not know what the future holds for me in ministry. I do believe that as time goes on life will get a little easier for women clergy, and I trust that I will be able to continue doing the ministry that God is calling me to do.

Susan Storey

My ordination as deacon in October 1987, and as priest in February 1988, was the culmination for me of a long process of testing, questioning, doubting, and affirming. It was in 1975 in New York State, when I first encountered a woman priest, that the possibility of being ordained myself first seriously crossed my mind. However, since, as I told myself, I had no desire to be either an object of curiosity or a martyr, I did not pursue the idea. I did begin work on an M.Div. in Toronto in 1978 (and in 1981 on a Th.D.), but my stated aim was to prepare to teach theology. I never felt I entirely closed the door to ordained ministry, but neither did I pursue it.

During these years of theological study I struggled with issues of clerical authority, for example, as evidenced in special clergy privileges, titles, and garb. I struggled too with what it meant to be a dedicated lay person in the church. Increasingly, I became convinced I could not remain a lay person, but neither did I feel I could, in conscience, become part of what I perceived to be an enclave of patriarchal privilege — the ranks of the Anglican clergy. Working with a Korean priest in a small, ethnically and racially mixed parish in Toronto, and coming in contact with others who shared some of my views on clericalism, I gradually resolved the tensions between my strong sense of vocation and my grave doubts about the possibilities of working in ministry within the Anglican system. My love for a church that was highly sacramental, respectful of human reason and the work of theology, and concerned with issues of social justice also helped keep me within the Anglican fold.

The decision to seek ordination immediately involved for me two other decisions. First, should I remain in Canada, or return to my country of citizenship, the United States? Then, having decided in favour of Canada, where, exactly, should I go? My search for a diocese that was located in a section of the country where I would enjoy living, that needed clergy, and that welcomed ordained women led me to the diocese of Qu'Appelle. A few days after I was ordained deacon, I left Toronto in a rented truck and headed for Saskatchewan and my first parish.

Whitesand, a six-point parish in east central Saskatchewan, had all the frustrations of a large, multi-point parish. I found myself concentrating on the fundamentals — holding regular services and providing basic pastoral care. Considerable time had to be spent on the road. There were also joys and rewards: working with people who loved the church and took an active share in its ministry; the great privilege of working with an Indian congregation (the church has much to learn from them, I think); seeing a few new people coming to church; the faithfulness of long-time members; the country itself, beautiful in all its seasons.

Marriage to a fellow priest two years into my time in Whitesand parish meant difficult decisions and major changes. My husband's parish was even larger than mine and in need of a second priest, so I moved to Big Country parish on Saskatchewan's western border. Being part of a clergy couple had both advantages and drawbacks. Work-life and personal life became hard to separate; the transition from being "our priest" to also being "our priest's wife" was difficult. Nevertheless, working only part-time in the parish allowed me to complete a doctoral dissertation, and to teach ethics for a term at the College of Emmanuel and St. Chad in Saskatoon.

Parish work, dissertation writing, and teaching proved to be an exhausting combination. Yet this new opportunity for academic activities let me return to an old passion for intellectual life and work. The completion of the doctorate in theology in the spring of 1991 has opened up new possibilities for ministry in the years ahead.

At present my energies are channelled into parish work, diocesan ecumenical and interfaith committee work, CLAD (Canadian Lutheran/Anglican Dialogue), some retreat/quiet day leadership, and a varied program of reading. Whatever form it takes, the practice of ordained ministry is central to my life. Yet I do not see ministry, in any form, as an individualistic endeavour, but as inherently relational. It must be rooted in the church, carried out in a mutuality of relationships and ministries in the church and the world, and rooted in Jesus Christ, the vine of whom we are the branches.

Lynette Kent

If I have discussed the call to ordination with fifty clergy, forty-nine have indicated that it came gradually like dawn creeping over the prairie. My own call was more of an astral collision putting the Richter scale out of commission. It ocurred on 30 June 1977, the day before my tenth wedding anniversary. It was the culmination of months of a mysterious malady characterized by copious tears and complete bewilderment.

I was born in the midst of World War II in a little English town north of London. My upbringing was traditional. My church habits were completely predictable — Sunday School, confirmation, and more or less total rebellion against organized anything. This rebellion lasted until my marriage to Nick and the birth of our only daughter, Jennifer. Then began the second round of conformity. Our church was a charismatic (and dead-set-against-women priests) congregation. It was there, as I worked as a part-time secretary, that my life began to fall apart for no discernible reason. Then God hit me square between the eyes with a revelation that sent me into shock.

It was more than three years before I began to get over the effects. By that time, I had finished a B.Th. at Newman College, near Edmonton. It was another year before a posting was offered in Burns Lake, B.C., with four or five far-flung points. The parish was typical of any small town and the little congregations grew slowly but steadily. The tensions which existed within the parish families were typical of any other Christian church. But the core group was committed, and various types of lay ministry sprang up. It was a challenge I relished and, in spite of the conflict with family life and obligations and the heavy workload, Nick and I felt that it was the right place to be.

In early 1985, our lives were turned upside down by a drunk driver on a lonely highway. I was returning from a meeting in Prince George late one evening, and narrowly avoided being hit head-on by the driver who was using my lane. Her injuries were none and mine seemed minimal — a dislocated hip and numerous contusions, but the car was a write-off. So, it turned out, was my emotional well-being. A sudden, unexpected noise triggered a collapse that left me unable to function as a parish priest. By the end of 1985, it was obvious that the emotional breakdown would not improve soon enough to retain the incumbency. My family and I chose to return to Edmonton, and it was another two years before I could claim to have returned to normal. My family is still suffering from the effects.

A lawsuit claimed damages for the emotional damage as well as the physical injuries. The insurance company spent the next couple of years attempting to show that, because I was a woman in the stressful occupation of priest, and because I was so committed to the task, I was scheduled for a nervous breakdown anyway. Thanks to my lawyer's bulldog tenacity and good Scottish common sense, we went the whole distance. It became obvious that the issue was not the money but my suitability for the priesthood. Thanks to the testimony of my bishop, several psychiatrists, and friends, the court ruled that the accident alone had been the cause of the breakdown. It was a heady victory but a hollow one.

For the past seven years, I have applied for literally hundreds of positions. Several times, I have been the runner-up. I continue to spend my days working for the federal government and my spare time as occasional civilian chaplain in the Armed Forces and honorary assistant at a city church. It cannot begin to satisfy the longing I have to be fully involved in the life of a parish, able to counsel and teach and offer what talents I have. It leaves me with much the same feeling I have experienced since the loss of the first of three infants born after Jennifer — an ache and an emptiness that never completely disappears.

Patsy Ann Schmidt

My parish is St. Peter's on the Waskaganish Cree Reserve where the Rupert River and James Bay meet in Northern Quebec. The village is isolated. There are no roads leading out of the village. We can get out by river in the summer and by snow machine in the winter. There are flights six days a week. During late spring and late autumn, when the ice is not safe, some people use a helicopter to get to and from their bush camps and trap lines. Two-thirds of my small congregation live in the bush at least nine months of the year. They hunt, trap, and fish. In the spring, they bring the stretched and dry fur into the Hudson Bay Company store to earn money for supplies to go back into the bush for another year.

My parish is the oldest one on the Bay. I am the first woman priest they have had. My work is the same as any other parish priest's. First, I must love the people. I must feed them the spiritual food of the gospel and teach them to feed it to others. The village has 1300 souls. Seventy-five percent of them have been Pentecostal for eighteen years. The other 25 percent is divided between Roman Catholic, Anglicans, Northern Evangelicals and the non-churched. Six percent are Anglican and at least 5 percent attend Sunday services either in the village or hold their own in the bush camps. I must be with them in their day-to-day Christian journey as well as in their times of crisis — the deaths of loved ones, the lack of food. I have experienced the Cree people as deeply spiritual, both privately and communally.

I went back to school at the age of 42. I had only a Grade 8 education but, in four years, I earned my B.A. and M.Div. at Queen's University, Kingston. I was called to the priesthood many years ago but my parish priest at that time told me, ''The church does not ordain women." At that moment, I realized that I was different from men. I left the church. I was married, gave birth to three girls, was divorced, remarried, and I rediscovered God. God led me back into the church, opened the doors to schooling and ordination, rekindled the missionary spirit within me.

In this culture, which is not my own, I feel accepted by both women and men. I am trying very hard with my congregation to discover the living Christ within their own God-given spirituality, though much of this spirituality was lost through white man's Christianity. My greatest frustration comes from envious white women and male priests who don't know what it means to be the "image of Christ." They still really believe that it means having a penis.

I thank God that we have a primate who believes in the call of God to priesthood for both women and men, and in the importance of inclusive language. No longer is God addressed just as "Father," but "Mother" and "Creator." Jesus is "Sustainer," and our wonderful female Holy Spirit, "Wisdom," "Guide," and "Sanctifier."

It takes time. I pray that my granddaughters will grow up in a world where it will seem natural for a woman to be archbishop of Canterbury. The question of gender will not even be a factor in selection to that office.

My greatest learning as a priest comes from the realization that I am a role model, given the awesome task of caring for a small group of sheep who depend on me to do what is right. The more they see that I am human, with faults like them, the more we are able to journey together hand in hand. The question is not if we are female or male priests. We will be judged by how we loved the people of our congregations.

* * *

My husband became ill and on 30 November 1991 I moved back to Kingston, Ontario. I am, at the present time, part-time Anglican chaplain at Kingston General Hospital and chaplain to the Cree people who come to Kingston for medical care.

Peggy Sheffield

I did not seek to be ordained. There was never a time in my life when I set out actively to pursue this course. When I finished four years of secondary-school education in England in 1936, and indeed throughout my teenage years until that time, my one desire was to be a missionary. To some extent this was fostered by a Sunday School teacher who had done missionary work abroad, and I was an avid reader of the *Torch* series of booklets on the lives of missionaries.

However, as a child of working-class parents there was no opportunity in those days for young people such as I to take the training for such work, unless one was fortunate enough to find a generous benefactor.

I do not remember ever sharing my ambition with my parents. Because it seemed such an unreachable goal it seemed better to keep it to myself, and in due course I embarked on a secretarial career. Little did I guess at that time how my early ambition would come to fruition in a very different way, and late in life, and that it would be, and still is, a great joy. When God closes one door, he opens another, if we only have the eyes of faith to see it.

My late husband was a lay reader in charge of a small parish for twenty-two years. Following his death in 1974 there was no one able or willing to carry on the work. The small congregation feared that once the door of the church closed, it would never open again, so I volunteered to become lay reader in charge until other arrangements could be made. At that time I had four children still at home and a garage business which kept me working full time until I sold it three years later.

Seven years later I was still lay reader in charge. I worked part time keeping books for three local businesses to augment my income, and spent my spare time doing parish work. I had, without realizing it, become a pastor, but unable to fulfil pastoral duties. The regional dean travelled eighty-five miles every other month to bring us Holy Communion after her own services were over for the day.

Because of my work I identified closely with the diocesan clergy and attended deanery chapter meetings, although I was not, of course, included in retreats or clergy workshops. This began to cause problems for me. I wanted to be one *with* the clergy, but not *of* them.

Why was this? I had lived and worked in the same community since coming to Canada in 1946. I was well-known, took a very active part in small-town, rural life, enjoyed the respect of some people and the friendship of many. I didn't want a change in status that might threaten this. I didn't want suddenly to be regarded as ''different.'' Ordination would affect my relationship with my family. No more week-end visits with children and grandchildren. What would happen at Christmas time? I was very involved in the Diocesan Lay Readers Association, and reluctant to make a move that would, no doubt, change that relationship.

A few members of the diocesan clergy, and especially two ordained women, suggested on more than one occasion that I should seriously consider ordination. The bishop at that time, the Rt Revd John Conlin, also suggested it in 1981. It would be two more years before I gave up the struggle against ordination, and a further year before I was ordained. Once the decision was made I felt a great sense of relief and peace.

As it turned out I need not have worried so much about the local reaction. I decided to ignore any awkwardness I encountered, and for the most part it disappeared in a fairly short time. Many people mistakenly assumed that I had passed a lot of tough academic examinations. I had been taking courses by correspondence, off-campus courses, and a week at St. John's College, Winnipeg each summer, all of which I found essential in order to be able to carry out my role as lay reader in the parish, but my decision to be ordained was not the culmination of a course of study. People were eager to congratulate me on having achieved something in the academic sense, but had little or no appreciation for my struggle with the loss of my former identity, and the resultant sacrifices that would be necessary with regard to my family and my other community pursuits.

Eventually my congregation joined with another six-point parish, and I began working in a team ministry with a younger male priest. At first we experimented with rotating all seven points for services, but this proved to be costly and time-wasting, and it was impossible for one person to visit in seven different communities, so we divided the parish east and west for the purpose of services. Several times a year we exchanged pulpits so that we both kept in touch with all congregations, and several times a year representatives of all congregations met at regular intervals for Parish Council meetings. Once the other priest and I had come to terms with our different styles of churchmanship, the difference in our outlook because of age, and agreed to disagree about some things, the relationship worked well, and continued for six years.

I have experienced some of the same frustrations as all clergy, both male and female: the parochial attitude of congregations; diocesan and national church directives that bear little relationship to life in *tiny* rural congregations; the lack of perception of the all-encompassing nature of a priest's work in the rural setting (no secretary or photocopier); dwindling and dispirited congregations. At times I get very impatient with the institutional church. We get bogged down in legalism and nit-picking that seems far removed from the propagation of the gospel. This is much more evident to me as a priest than it was as a lay reader. When I began taking theological courses I was amazed and irritated that so little of the insights afforded by scholarship appear in Sunday morning sermons and Bible studies.

Before I was ordained I knew that a very few of the diocesan clergy were not in favour of women priests. One of the examining chaplains could not act in my case for that reason. However, I have been fortunate that on no occasion have I been treated really unkindly. The few times I have detected condescension it has come from an academic, rather than a male, sense of superiority. On the other hand, the provision of suitable clothing has been a constant problem. The people who produce women's clergy shirts and albs seem to have little knowledge of female contours. As for cassocks, a clerk in Gaspard's once told me apologetically, "We just don't have cassocks to suit your anatomy!" Thus I have never owned a cassock, and have made my own shirts and dresses, experimenting with the collar until I got it right.

If the people in my first congregation had doubts about a woman in the pulpit, they did not let it show, and whole-heartedly supported my ordination, so long as it didn't mean they would lose me!

On the plus side, I now have very dear friends in five or six more rural communities, people for whom I am not just a parish priest. I have gained great satisfaction from my association with other clergy, both in and out of the diocese, and also of other denominations. I feel that my life has been greatly enriched by my work, in fact it has in a very real sense become my life. My family have been very supportive, encouraging, and understanding, although there are times when, because of my duties, I have not been able to do for them what I might have done in different circumstances.

What have I learned? Above all, I have learned that people matter more than anything else. That where we give the cup of love, it is returned to us pressed down and running over. I have learned to do what God calls me to do and to leave the results to him. I have had profound conversations with non-churchgoers, and have learned how mistaken we are when we believe that such people are lacking in spirituality. Last, but by no means least, I have learned that whenever we look for, or anticipate, trouble, insults, put-downs, we are likely to find them. It has been a male-dominated world for a very long time. Old habits die hard. We all, men and women, need time to adjust to a totally different way of viewing sexuality. Patient persistence will get us further than confrontation. Honey works better than vinegar! It is God, and not people, who bless, or withhold blessing, on our efforts to spread the gospel.

I have now reached the end of my time as an active priest,

although I remain an honorary assistant, and am active in other ways in the diocese. It has been for me a time of hard work, a time of hope, a time of fulfilment, and more than anything else a time of joy.

I am certain that it is God's will that women should be ordained, and that the years to come will vindicate this belief. God made us male and female. We bring to life different attributes, intuitions, perceptions, and values. We complement each other. Both are needed to nurture the Body of Christ. Together we make up the People of God.

Virginia Briant

The twentieth of December 1988 began for me just like any other work day. I planned to deliver Christmas presents in North Vancouver, take communion to a very frail man in Deep Cove, and then celebrate with my husband, Bob, our thirty-ninth wedding anniversary. First I had to see my doctor over by the university. On the way back to North Vancouver, I woke up in an ambulance with someone sticking a needle into my hand and someone else cutting off my clothes. I was in and out of consciousness for two days but learned that someone had lost control of his car and hit me head on. My whole right side from the top of my head to my foot had been terribly hurt, but I was alive and I would walk again. So began a long time of recovery. While I was in hospital, cards, flowers, visitors, and phone calls rolled in. I had messages from people I could not even remember. I thanked God for all the love and concern poured out on me, and I knew that my life had not been wasted. I have had a great deal of time to pray, study, meditate, and reflect on my sixteen years in the ordained ministry.

It began in 1964 when I was confirmed along with my elder son and my husband at St. John's Episcopal Church in Ketchikan, Alaska. I felt that touch of the Lord upon my shoulder. For the next six years I studied my Bible and religious books, prayed, and yearned to serve God. Finally God began to open doors. In 1970 Canada began to ordain women to the diaconate, as I began studies at the Vancouver School of Theology. In 1973 General Synod voted for the first time to ordain women to the priesthood, the same year I graduated with an M.Div. degree, was ordered deacon, and went on the staff of Christ Church Cathedral, Vancouver. General Synod voted a second time in 1975 and the date of 30 November 1976 was set for the first ordinations of women in Canada. In my three-and-a-half years of serving as a deacon, I had learned how necessary it was for my ministry to become a priest. My main responsibility was to care for the elderly, sick, and dying people. I needed to hear confessions and then give absolution and blessings. How much I desired to celebrate the Holy Eucharist. The day finally came when I, along with five other women in Canada, became a priest in the church of God.

The next five years were spent in ministry, in pastoral care, and establishing a healing ministry at Christ Church Cathedral. In 1981 I became a rector of St. Richard's, North Vancouver. While on medical leave, I had time to work on my photo album. The pictures helped me to remember with great appreciation some of the beautiful and blessed moments in my ministry.

I married the daughter of a beautiful woman who was dying of cancer. I had been beside Doreen's hospital bed when she was so ill. I had seen her lose all her hair and listen to her many concerns about the family she dearly loved. I almost broke down on the night of the wedding when I saw Doreen, on a pass from the hospital, looking radiant. She had on a silver wig and a lovely dress and was beautiful. What love for her family had wrought!

Another wedding which touched me deeply was that of a Canadian groom and a Japanese bride. I shared the service with a Japanese priest. I read the vows to the groom in English and the other priest read the vows in Japanese to the bride.

The greatest thrill of all is to bring children and adults into the Body of Christ through baptism — the family of nine baptized together, an East Indian lad from a Muslim family, many babies and small children. I become misty-eyed every time I give communion to these same children and see their tiny hands reaching out to receive the body of Christ.

Many other beautiful events come to mind — the tears of joy from people who have gone through confession and found blessed relief from their sins and regrets — the prayers beside hospital beds — preaching at Christmas and Easter — the tenth anniversary of my ordination to the priesthood when the basement of St. Richard's was full of butterflies made by my people

— the healing services when I knew people were touched by God in real and meaningful ways. God has truly blessed me with so many wonderful experiences.

What do women bring to priesthood? I think the most important thing we bring is the completion of the Image of God. He created us in his image — male and female he created us. How wonderful for men and women to share in ministry — at the altar, at weddings, at funerals, and in counselling.

A prayer that means much to me and one I pray each day:

The Prayer of St. Richard of Chichester:
Thanks be to thee O Lord Jesus Christ for all the benefits which thou hast given us.
For all the pains and insults which thou hast borne for us.

I, too, have suffered in his ministry but there is nothing I have experienced that our Lord had not known in a much more terrible way.

O merciful Redeemer, friend and brother,
May I see Thee more clearly,
Follow Thee more nearly,
Love Thee more dearly now and for evermore. Amen.

Now I remember what had called me through the many years of frustration before I entered seminary — my desire to serve the Lord, my longing to help others come to know him. I thank God that he has deemed me worthy to follow him. I will not be spared sufferings but will be given the grace, power, protection, and love to do what he would have me do.

* * *

Due to head and foot injuries I was forced to take early retirement. But I do enjoy being retired and I still have several ministries. I am a better housewife and have more time for my family. Also I am able to take some services at the local Anglican churches in this area. I am chaplain for the Order of St. Luke which gives me enough pastoral and teaching experiences to satisfy my desire to continue to serve our Lord.

Hagar Head

I was born in The Pas, Manitoba, and am a Native person from the Swampy Cree nation. I was ordained as an Anglican priest by our late bishop, the Right Reverend John Conlin, on 3 July 1990. Presently I am enrolled in the Vancouver School of Theology taking my Master of Divinity degree through correspondence.

When I first got ordained, I sensed the loneliness. I think that the people in our community didn't know how to react to a woman priest. But, within our culture, we have always been taught that there were holy women around us before the European culture was introduced to us.

During my training in ministry, I began to realize that the turmoil I went through was for a purpose. It made me grow stronger in my faith. This was when I found my Lord and Saviour. My eyes were opened. I had to look at myself and start moving towards tomorrow.

I have many roles in ministry:

— being a daughter
— being a mother
— being a wife
— being a daughter-in-law
— being a mother-in-law
— being a grandmother
— being a sister-in-law
— being an assistant priest
— being a chaplain at the Correctional Institution in The Pas, Manitoba
— being a half-time teacher at the Henry Budd Centre in The Pas.

As a Native person and a woman, I feel strongly that my personal story of ministry is not an accident. God the Creator has a reason for everything on earth. Women have a major role on earth. Native culture respects women because they bring life, giving birth to children. Christ gave his life for all so we can have new birth.

Rae Kiebuzinski

I am a widow and a priest, and never in my wildest dreams did I ever expect to become a priest. When Jesus called me into his service, I was prepared to give him all my time, love, loyalty, and strength. I became a full-time parish worker but constantly felt I was not doing enough. I got up earlier, worked later at night — all to no avail. Finally, exhausted, I got down on my knees and said, "Lord, what more can I do?" His answer was prompt. "Be ordained as a priest." I had a lot of problems with this idea, because I believed that I was the wrong sex, the wrong age (60), and too much of a sinner to be worthy of so great an honour. However, God's prodding continued until I applied to my bishop for ordination. Then peace reigned. I went smoothly through the process of selection and further education.

I was given the responsibility of two parishes forty-five miles apart, Red Lake and Ear Falls. I had already lived for thirty years in Ear Falls. I soon learned to cope with emotional contrasts. On the day I was to be ordained deacon, a snowstorm prevented the bishop from coming, so the ordination was postponed to the following day. This meant not only that my out-of-town friends who had already taken a day off work were not at the ceremony, but also that it fell on the same day that I had agreed to conduct a funeral following the sudden death of a young mother whom I had known since childhood.

There are two major difficulties in this area. One is the distances which separate our scattered population. The Red Lake district is divided into two townships, both encompassing settlements originally built around gold mines. Each township is bigger than Ear Falls, so most of my work is in this northern area. The highway between parishes is lonely and crosses isolated bush country. It is paved and in good condition in the summer, but, in winter, weather and road conditions are often poor. One Christmas Eve, following the late service, I did not meet another car all the way from Red Lake to Ear Falls. I bought a car with front-wheel drive and the Ear Falls A.C.W. gave me a C.B. radio for my car.

My other difficulty was a transient population which frustrated the first five years of my ministry. People came to the north to earn money, not to stay. In 1986, an iron mine north of Ear Falls closed. About 200 homes became vacant as people found work elsewhere. Our congregation was depleted and the vestry cut in half. On the plus side, men out of work spent time completing the interior of our parish hall. The following year the core congregation in Red Lake took some losses as people left the area for more lucrative jobs. We lost two layreaders, the Sunday School superintendent, a warden, and the organist. So there was continual need for training and education. In Red Lake I trained three groups of servers in three years and was still left a year later with no server.

When there is this movement of population, community building is difficult. The entire congregation grieves these losses. The theology of bringing the newly baptized into a Christian community was a theory, not a reality. During a baptism, I would wonder whether the family would still be in town by the time the child was old enough to attend Sunday School. I would have felt better about the loss of these families if I had known they were going out into the wider world with a sense of mission, to continue their ministry. Unfortunately, this did not seem to be the case. A transient life seems a disrupted one.

This lack of permanence may explain why there is still no Anglican church building in the Red Lake district. We rent time in the Roman Catholic church. We work by the clock and do not experience the timelessness of a northern reservation. One Sunday morning, I had a native baptism scheduled. The family never showed up. When our service was over and the Roman Catholics were arriving, the baptismal party arrived. I had to leave for the service in Ear Falls and had to ask them to postpone the baptism for another week. I felt badly about this because they did not understand.

During the past three years of my ministry here the situation has changed. There is more permanence to the population, which may be due to lack of employment elsewhere in Canada. Consequently, community building has been possible and both parishes have experienced a strong sense of belonging to the larger Christian family which worships and works together in love.

My aim has been to bring people to know and love Jesus Christ as their Lord and Saviour with the resulting baptism of the Holy Spirit. When beginning my ministry I thought the best way to achieve this was to pull people out of the secular world for a brief time, so that they might be still and know that Christ was with them. I encouraged them to attend Cursillo weekends, silent retreats, Vacation Bible Schools, Summer Bible Camps.

Due to the considerable growth of the Red Lake district while I have been priest-in-charge, this year the Diocesan Council arranged funding to have a full-time priest resident there. The parish chose another woman priest, the Reverend Nancy Selwood. She began her ministry on 1 June 1992. This has left me with only one parish and less travel, which has enabled me to concentrate my time and energies in Ear Falls where the numbers now worshipping together fill our little church building on a Sunday morning. Working with me are a strong team of committed Christians who assist with parish ministry to both young and old. The bond of love which unites us is a force which attracts other families into our Christian community. To experience the Holy Spirit working in other peoples' lives is both humbling and rewarding.

As a World War II veteran, I am pleased to be chaplain of the Ear Falls Legion branch. My personal weekly highlight is sermon preparation. I feel I cannot witness too often, both to bring new people to Christ and to feed committed Christians. In preparation for my departure from the parish (I am now over seventy years old) we have formed a small Education for Ministry group to train future non-stipendiary priests for ministry.

Throughout my long and varied life, I have worked at many occupations. My work as parish priest is the most fulfilling I have ever experienced. I praise and thank God continually that he has taken me into his service. It is a life I can thoroughly recommend because Jesus Christ gives us the courage and all gifts necessary to equip us and empower us to accomplish the job.

Ann Cheetham

Prior to ordination, I was a music teacher, pianist, and organist, trained in the strict classical tradition. I had been teaching for twenty-six years when I felt a call to the ordained ministry. My piano and theory classes were both very large and included some quite brilliant talent. At that time I was one of three teachers in Saskatoon who taught advanced theory and diploma work. I had just upgraded my studio with the purchase of a new piano. However, early in my adult life, I had prayed for guidance and promised to serve my Lord in whatever way he chose. The church had always been a large part of my family's life. I grew up in the Junior Choir and JA. Later I served on vestry for many years. When I realized that I was being called into full-time, ordained ministry, I gradually let my students go as I proceeded through my studies at the College of Emmanuel and St. Chad, Saskatoon. I was ordered deacon on the Feast of St. Boniface, 5 June 1986, and was ordained priest the following year on 28 April.

I served as Diocesan Hospital Chaplain in Saskatoon, centering my work on the three general hospitals in the city where I visited and ministered to the need of Anglican patients from outside the city. As Saskatoon is the principal medical centre for the province, the hospitals have large numbers of patients from other centres. I trained lay, Pastoral Care, volunteer visitors and co-ordinated their work. I enjoyed the fellowship of the chaplains and sisters of other denominations. My office was located in a parish church. My predecessors worked from offices in a hospital or in the Synod Office, but I asked the bishop for an office in a parish. I felt that I needed a parish base rather than a hospital one to discourage any attempt to identify myself with one hospital when my responsibilities were in all three. I feel that hospital chaplains can easily become divorced from the everyday life of a parish. I feel that it is in the parish that the church is most vital and active and alive. It is in the parish that our Lord's work is being done — in the secular community, by the Christian community which makes its home in the parish. I served as honorary assistant in the same parish and worked as a team with the rector and his wife, both priests of the diocese.

I served as hospital chaplain for four years. That is probably as long as I feel that I should stay in that work at any one time. Unless the chaplain has a strong link with a parish, he or she can easily develop an unbalanced perspective. Hospital life is *not* normal life for the patient. Parish life is normal. Work as chaplain is very rewarding, but it is very draining, often intense, and very sad. It is an area of ministry where being a woman is a distinct advantage. A female chaplain can comfort a bereaved parent or spouse with a hug more easily and naturally than can a man.

In 1990, I moved to the diocese of Qu'Appelle as incumbent of a multi-point, rural parish. It has been a great change for me. I had never before lived in a small town. The town is entirely dependent on the surrounding farms and is feeling the adverse effects of our depressed rural economy and shrinking population. But the people here are strong, compassionate towards one another, kindly, and generous. I am very aware of the richness and variety of wildlife, which makes living in southern Saskatchewan a real delight. There is an abundance of birds and I frequently see deer or pronghorn or coyotes or foxes as I travel on parish business. For the first time in my life, I am living alone — with my three cats and dog.

I serve as half-time priest and half-time music teacher. This town has not had a professional music teacher for many years. Being a "country person" is a dream come true. I have found ministering in this setting very rewarding. I am able to get close to people, to minister to them where they are, and to encourage them to exercise the ministry of their baptism. This is a very small town with two other denominations, United and Free Methodist. The surrounding towns have Roman Catholic congregations and Roumanian Orthodox. We are happily interdenominational, with good fellowship and friendships among the people and clergy and religious. There are some things we had in the city that we don't have here. There is no choir. Midweek activities are kept to a minimum because of the distances people have to travel. Most of the parishioners have livestock and looking after the animals must take priority, especially at calving time.

Being an ordained person in the church has many more pluses than minuses. It is an extremely busy life and, if I were married, I would need to work very hard to make sure enough time was given to family and home. As it is, I have difficulty finding time for myself and the family commitments I do have. Clergywomen are still few in number but I personally have not felt discriminated against. There are some people, both clergy and lay, who have not yet come to terms with the idea of women in the ordained ministry, but that is their problem, not mine. People who were strongly against the ordination of women have now, since my ordination and since we have come to know one another better, become good friends and respected colleagues. The frustrations that bother me are those common to other clergy — not enough time to do what we need to do, not enough pastoral care for the pastors. I have never considered myself a feminist or part of the women's movement. I dislike controversy but am prepared to take a stand — as a person, as a child of God, not as a woman per se. God calls both men and women to serve him. I am a priest in love with my work, in love with my Lord and in love with his church.

Alice Medcof

My parents came from Europe after the First World War —
my mother was of Polish and Ukrainian descent, and my
father of Czechoslovakian and German descent. They met in
Toronto, married, and lived in the inner city while my father
established his own plumbing and heating business. When I was
four, we moved to North York. We maintained our contacts with
the ethnic community by visiting on weekends our friends and
family. My mother and godmother tried to bring me up in the
Roman Catholic Church but distance made regular church attendance chancy. The Anglican Church of St. Philip the Apos-
tle was nearby. Through weekday activities I developed a happy
relationship with members of the church and, at age 16, decided to seek confirmation in the Anglican church. Upon graduation from the University of Toronto, I took a job as a
programmer-analyst with KCS Limited, the first Toronto firm
to have a business computer. In 1958 I married James Medcof.
We adopted our daughter Cathi in 1964 and our son Bill in 1967.

Jamie and I had agreed that, if we had a family, I would give
up my job until the youngest child was in school all day. When
the children were young, I joined the University Women's Club
and, through their activities, was introduced to the world of social action. The women met to study particular issues in depth
and, from time to time, a member would find her vocation, either
volunteer or paid, as a result. I thought a great deal about this
but their answers were not adequate for me because of the
predominantly humanistic orientation. I felt that such work would
be so much more satisfying and successful if a Christian base were
consciously affirmed as a way of helping people achieve a fuller
life. I decided that it was time to pick up a latent interest, church

history, and enrolled as an occasional student in the Faculty of Divinity at Trinity College. During that year, I became convinced that my future career would be church oriented, though the exact job description was far from clear.

When General Synod agreed to ordain women, the diocesan authorities put me provisionally in the ordination stream. Field placements convinced me that God's goal for me was ordained ministry. I was ordained deacon on 18 May 1979 and priested on 18 May 1980. I served my curacy at St. Paul's, Lorne Park, then went to Christ Church, Deer Park as priest associate. In 1983, I was made incumbent of the Church of the Epiphany, and in 1987, of St. Bede's, Scarborough. I am presently incumbent of the Church of the Transfiguration, Toronto. In 1990 I received my Th.M. degree.

In addition to parish ministry, my work has included chaplaincy, student supervision, and women's concerns with emphasis on the global networking of women. Highlights have included designing a course for and training lay pastoral visitors for Mississauga Hospital, attending the World Council of Churches Assembly (Vancouver, 1983), and attending General Synod 1983 as part of the Women's Unit presentations. While at Synod, I had the privilege of being the first woman to celebrate the eucharist for the entire assembly. In April 1986, the Movement for the Ordination of Women held a Service of Thanksgiving for the Ministry of Women Throughout the Ages, in Canterbury Cathedral, at which women from twenty-two countries were present. Of these, fourteen were selected to meet with the archbishop of Canterbury, Robert Runcie, to discuss the variety of women's ministries in the Anglican church. Canada was represented by the Revd Sister Rosemary Anne Benwell and myself. This was the first time that the archbishop had invited an international group of ordained women to speak with him.

From July 1986 to August 1987, I joined my husband on his sabbatical leave in London, England. The Movement for the Ordination of Women, and Women in Theology, were my chief support groups as I coped with the ambiguity of knowing myself to be a priest but being unable to authenticate that in action amongst people who yearned for the sacramental ministry of a woman. Preaching, though, was allowed and I enjoyed the opportunities to preach in various parts of England. Spiritual highlights of that year were: being in Bethlehem for Christmas and in Spain for Holy Week, retreats in a Quaker Centre, being with the community on Iona, and the Taizé community.

In June 1988, my name was on the ballot for an episcopal election, and in July of that year I joined women from around the world who formed the Women's Witnessing Community at the Lambeth Conference. One of the women was the future Bishop Barbara Harris. In February 1989 several of us attended her consecration in Boston. In March 1992 I attended Anglican Encounter in Brazil. I have been a member of the National Executive Council, the Program Committee, and the Women's Unit, and am presently on the Toronto Diocesan Executive Committee.

I look forward to the future confident that the Holy Spirit will continue to lead women and men in an atmosphere of justice and equality.

Margaret Amy Marquardt

In 1975, two particularly important things happened to me. I took part in an ecumenical women's group to plan a weekend gathering — Women of the Covenant. It was through this process that a new understanding of liturgy, scripture, and the role of women in the church began to emerge for me. Secondly, for Christmas I received Letty Russel's book, *Human Liberation from a Feminist Perspective*, from a co-worker. For the first time I began to wonder if I could study theology and possibly be ordained to the priesthood. I was so excited about Letty Russel's view of faithful ministry. She named the oppression of women, their exclusion from leadership in religious bodies, and the new contribution they could bring as part of human liberation. This resonated with me since I was already connected with women's concerns through the Women's Liberation Movement of the early 1970s, and with issues of poverty through my own family history, living and working in inner-city Winnipeg, with my B.A. in Urban Studies. I began to see how I could connect my faith with a vocation.

In 1975, I was still a Roman Catholic but attending St. Matthew's Anglican Church, which was part of an ecumenical ministry with Maryland United Church. I was working as a Community Worker with St. Matthews-Maryland Community Ministry. It was an early morning, contemporary, eucharist service that brought me into the Anglican church. The eucharist has always been a central part of my worship life, because it breaks through our logic and grounds us in the everyday life of the community, of bread and wine, of all having enough food to eat, none going hungry, and none excluded from the table. We gather in our brokenness, connecting to the broken and living body of Christ in the world.

In 1976, I was received into the Anglican Church of Canada at St. Matthew's by the rector, the Revd David Crawley. I attended the Vancouver School of Theology from 1977–1980, graduating with my Master of Divinity. It was there that I learned about the contextual approach to scripture, so that I could preach, seeking to understand the various societies out of which scripture arose. This is especially important in looking with fresh eyes about the use of scripture as weapon against women, and those on the sidelines of society. I was ordained to the diaconate 18 October 1980, and the priesthood 1 November 1981 in the diocese of Rupert's Land by the Rt Revd Barry Valentine. I began by serving as a curate in Selkirk, Manitoba and on the Scanterbury Indian Reserve. It was difficult and I was not equipped to deal with the disintegration of the Anglican church on the reserve and the growing power of fundamentalism. After one-and-a-half years, my curacy was completed and I moved to Vancouver with the prospect of a position as an assistant at a parish.

Unfortunately, the situation changed and the position did not materialize. I was in the very difficult position of being newly ordained, not known in the diocese of New Westminster and therefore a risk for anyone to take on, still one of relatively few women clergy, desiring to remain in urban ministry, and strongly committed to social justice and the concerns of women. I was not to have a full-time position in the church for three years. Even though I was not fully employed I did not waste those years. I did Sunday supply, led and co-ordinated workshops, volunteered in many different areas of the church and social change groups, and worked in 1984–85 as chairperson of The Peoples' Commission of Solidarity Coalition. The Commission was an outgrowth of a mass movement of unions and community groups that came together following the Provincial Budget of 1983 which decimated the funding for social services among other things. The Commission toured twelve communities in the province and heard from citizens about their solutions to address the political, economic, ecological, and social concerns of their region.

My time of unemployment, of not being able to find a church to serve in, as well as the experiences I had during the three years stay with me, and continue to teach me. There were some clergy, and a number of lay people, who were especially caring of me during this time. It was a painful time for I felt displaced and longed for a church community where I could serve.

Since 1985, I have been at St. Margaret's, Cedar Cottage, a small parish in Vancouver's east side; a vibrant, mixed-ethnic area of working-class roots with increasing poverty and social problems. St. Margaret's church and hall were destroyed by arson in 1980, and thus we worship in the former rectory, renovated for our purposes. The parish has been trying with diligence and considerable expense and obstacles to make wise use of our land. All has come together as of January 1993, with a definite plan of housing for persons suffering from mental illness, along with a new church and hall.

I feel very much at home in the congregation. People appreciate my leadership in liturgy and preaching which speaks of who we are, some of the struggles we have come from and still have as women and men, the concerns of the poor and those who are excluded in church and society, and what it is to receive the gifts of people whomever they are. We experiment in liturgy together, allowing the use of feminine images of God and images of the character of God and God's relationship with us, to teach us. I must take risks in order to be faithful, and find that I can share openly with the congregation about my ideas and proposals for ministry, and they with me. I see the need to continue to be self-critical about my role within the institution of the church. As a woman priest, I want to reflect on my own experiences as a woman as well as the situation of women in church and society and ask what this means for my leadership. It is important to me to seek out the voices of the suffering in their struggles and their hopes, and have this be a lens through which I look at my ministry. This kind of critique is also essential for the congregation. The focus of our liturgy and our parish life speaks of what we care about.

A prayer (copyright) from a work in progress by the Revd Kathleen Schmitt of the diocese of New Westminster (used with permission) speaks to what I pray and seek:

God Whom We Meet in One Another

We discover Christ crucified in the bagwoman on the
    street,
in our neighbour who dies unknown to us of AIDS,
and in the child who starves in lands both near and far.
We discover Christ risen in the strength of the survivors
    of abuse, exploitation and oppression,
and those who have learned to use evil for good and to
    turn hatred to love.
Through your church speak to us of the reconciliation
    promised before the foundations of the earth:
that the hearts of people everywhere know and love You
    for ever
in that world full of Your goodness that never ends;
Lover, Justice-Maker, Spirit of Redemption.

*

Vignettes

Ottawa

A Confessed Overachiever

She was an Olympic runner, a national record-holder, a professional artist and is still an unbeatable badminton player. She spent most of her life looking for God — almost never in a church. Then, one day, she met a priest who allowed her to ask all the questions to which everyone had said, "Shh!" He asked her if she would design a leaflet and on it depict the Holy Spirit.

"Do you have a picture for me to copy?"

"No."

This has caused her to ponder and to think long and hard. Suddenly she felt the presence of Jesus in a way she had never previously experienced, and she found herself saying, "I'll do anything you ask." The answer came in one word, "Priesthood."

It was a year before she summoned the courage to speak to anyone about this, and many years longer before she was ordained. Now that she is working as a priest, something of that restless spirit within her has found peace.

"I'm incredibly happy," she says.

Rejection Redeemed

It was a raw moment in the parish council meeting, as the group came to an impasse over a particular issue. She made what she thought was the obvious suggestion, "Why don't we pray about it?" The rector was incredulous. He could not understand why she would ask such a thing. She went home downhearted.

Then, over the next few days, she began to receive phone calls from fellow parishioners. "Don't give up," was their refrain. A day or so later, she was sitting in her living room, when she had a vision of Jesus saying, "Don't let anyone come between me and your walk to me."

One special aspect of her walk to Jesus was the sense that he was calling her to priesthood. She encountered many difficulties and challenges during the years of preparation. She was a single mother with teenagers to look after. She had to take time off work to study and had very little money. However, the bishop affirmed her throughout. When it seemed as though everyone else was doubting her call, he assured her that he had never doubted it. When the day finally came to preside at her first eucharist, she had the very strong feeling that she "belonged" there, behind the altar.

Today she is the rector of a rural parish. When she first arrived, she found several men who used their body language to intimidate her. But she stood her ground. She won their respect by showing that she meant what she said, and deserved to be heard. Now she is beginning to bring about, in the parish, changes close to her heart — lay participation in the liturgy, effective marriage preparation, and prayers for healing.

Priest and Mother

When she went to her ACPO assessment, one assessor advised her to stay home and have babies, and let her husband be the priest. Though she was very young, she summoned the courage to ask for an additional interview. This took place with a woman. She was held back one year but, in retrospect, believes this was probably to her own benefit, as it allowed her time to mature. Is there a *kairos* to being called? Does it happen at precisely the right time?

In spite of this, she was a year farther along than her husband because he had done other things before pursuing his theological education. She made the decision to delay ordination, partly because she and her husband would otherwise spend the year apart, and partly because they wanted to be ordained together. She received a lot of criticism for this, particularly from other women, which upset her very much.

Today she is the rector of a rural parish, their first woman rector. The first months were "not so much a honeymoon as a period of grace." After one year, a man said, "We were not sure of you and it wasn't because you are a woman. After all, our cows here are innoculated by a woman, and the milk collection truck is driven by a woman. I just want to tell you that you've been good for the men around here. I don't know though if you've been able to reach the women." His wife and daughter were listening. "You're wrong, Dad," his daughter said. "She's been very good for us too."

At the Easter Vigil, she baptized two little girls. The only way she could hold them was to rest them on her large, very pregnant abdomen, hoping her water would not break before the weekend was over. Her daughter was born shortly after. Following maternity leave, she resumed work in the parish on a part-time basis.

This woman's story kindled joyful thoughts for others in the group. One spoke with delight of the experience of giving a special blessing to pregnant women by touching their abdomen as they come forward to receive communion.

One Hundred and Fifty Percent

We talked about the need for women to give 150% of what is expected from a man in a similar position, just to establish credibility/capability. We experienced this as theology students and experience it still. For some, it seems worse when one is assistant in a parish where the rector is a "workaholic." We pondered the appropriateness of any position which requires someone to be at parish functions five or six nights a week. What sign is that of the wholeness of life in Christ? One woman had a miscarriage just before Christmas services. She conducted her services *before* allowing herself to be taken to hospital.

Who Is the Church?

One of the priests spent several years as rector of a "bedroom community," country parish before coming to be the assistant at the cathedral. While in a country parish, she was able to set out her days in a way that seemed good to her and to the people to whom she ministered. People were not keen to come to endless evening meetings, which suited her too! Most of her ministry was in people's homes, around the kitchen table, in the hospital and school. She was there not only to minister to her parishioners but to the community as well. Parish events were intergenerational and were often open to the whole community.

It was incredibly difficult to switch to the far more structured, office-bound position of assistant at the cathedral. She had the feeling of being part of something which, by its very corporate nature, clipped her creativity and snuffed her energy. On reflection, she could only hope that the presence of women in the priesthood would help to expand and bring new spirit to ministry, rather than limit the expression of women's — and men's — individual gifts of ministry.

Now this woman is in a diocesan community ministry, a new residence for women who have been homeless or who have special needs. People ask, "Why ever did you leave the cathedral to take a job like that? Aren't you wasting your education and experience?"

"In a very real way, this *is* my parish right now. Even though I must be wary of bringing religious language where that would be inappropriate, I am beginning to feel that I can now offer the love and healing of Christ to a group of women who would never dare belong to a conventional parish."

She hopes this experience will also allow her, as guest preacher in various parishes, to bring about a greater understanding of the long-hidden tragedy of poor and violated women.

"So Out of Sight, I'm Going Out of my Mind"

A priest works part time as chaplain on the palliative care team of one of Canada's largest hospitals. She is rarely seen, day or night, without her pager on her belt loop. She spends most of her time with dying people and their families, as well as with the professionals who work with them. She feels a particular call to minister to those who are dying of AIDS and has been instrumental in setting up a home for people in the final stages of the disease who find themselves without the support and care they need. She said most emphatically that one of the things that annoys her is the lack of recognition of her AIDS ministry among diocesan clergy, and the subsequent isolation in the work.

A Healing Touch

They stood at the bedside of an elderly woman dying of cancer, a priest and the pastoral visitor who accompanied her. Without any planning, the visitor (a trained nurse) began rubbing the woman's back with cream and generally soothing her. The priest followed suit, fixing the pillows and helping the woman into a more comfortable position. Between the two of them, they took care of the woman's physical needs in a very loving, gentle way. Afterwards, they took her hand to pray with her.

They wondered, in the course of this, if male counterparts would have felt free to do these things. One of the group, who works closely with AIDS patients, noted that her freedom and ability respecting the more practical aspects of care seemed to come naturally. "I can do this because of my years as a mother."

Like Stepping Off a Diving Board

One woman sitting at the table with us is not yet ordained. She is a postulant in her last year of theological studies. She is another high achiever. Before beginning her studies, she was national Campaign Director for the Liberal Party. Her office was just down the street from her parish church, a large, old, brick building which is a sanctuary to many destitute people in Ottawa. One day she spoke to the priest-in-charge of her parish of her persistent dis-ease, which was not soothed by fine clothes, lavish meals, and prestige. He asked, "Have you ever thought that your dis-ease might be a consequence of your disobedience to the call you have felt to ordination?" (The Hebrew word "to obey" means "to listen.")

She was shaken by his comment. Not long after, she gave up her job, her apartment, and lifestyle in order to pursue theological studies leading to ordination. "It was like stepping off a diving board when you're not even sure you can swim, hoping for all you're worth that God will catch you." Yet for all the fear it sometimes brought, this step was one she felt she could not refuse to make.

"Before I quit my job, my soul was dying within me. I was participating in my own crucifixion."

She is very pensive as she ponders what the future may hold. "I'll be forty when and if I am ordained. How will God use me in the church?"

Ruth Helenor Matthews

B orn in 1916 in Quebec City, was educated there. Attended Trinity Anglican Church, was accepted by the Women's Auxiliary as a Missionary Candidate, trained at The Anglican Womens Training College and accepted for missionary service in Yukon diocese by the Rt Revd Tom Greenwood and in 1954 went to serve there. Began as Superintendent of St. Agnes Hospital, Whitehorse, while waiting for a place to live, in Carcross, where the bishop wished to have St. Saviour's parish re-opened. I then went to Teslin and left the Yukon to return to Toronto for further studies in the summer of 1960.

Was the first woman to be an assistant in the parish of Vaudreille and was ordained a deaconess in 1964, where the Rt Revd Tom Greenwood preached the sermon. Then in 1973 I was ordained a deacon to serve in Gaspé, Que. Again the first woman to be made a deacon in the Province of Quebec. On 5 June 1977, I was the first woman to be ordained a priest, in the Ecclesiastical Province of Canada. And served as the first woman rector of St. George's Anglican Church in Drummondville, Que. I retired as rector of the parish of Danville, Que. at the end of October 1987, and have continued to serve as honorary assistant at Richmond, Que. in the parish of St. Anne's. And am still priest-in-charge of St. Mark's Acton Vale, a summer charge.

All that I do is a great privilege, for me to be still able to serve the Lord and his people.

When I look back on almost thirty-nine years of full-time ministry for the Lord, I sometimes wonder if it really happened. There have been times of great joy and times of loneliness, times of regret, but I always knew that I had been called by our Lord to serve him. With the power of the Holy Spirit, I went forth, for underneath were the everlasting arms, and with that knowledge, I could do all things through Christ who strengthened me, as Saint Paul said. I believe that there is still a great deal of opposition to women clergy, and I see and sense it in many areas. This has been frustrating. But then I see growth and this is encouraging. I am saddened to see and hear of women striving to get where they wish, believing it is their right. I hope in time they will feel that with patience and with confidence if they are truly called, and wait upon the Lord for his guidance, the doors will be opened for them to serve and be fully accepted.

*

Women from Other Countries

There have been a number of women who felt a call to priesthood and who saw little hope of that being fulfilled in their own country in the foreseeable future. Some of these women came to Canada to be ordained. The stories of four women, from England, South Africa, and Australia, are included here.

Lucy Reid

My story begins in England where I lived until 1984. I felt drawn to ordained ministry from my teens and, when I had a career advisory interview, I startled my counsellor by telling him that I wanted to be a priest. He suggested that I consider social work instead, but also gave me a pamphlet about women's ministry as deaconesses. It was not very appealing! However, with the optimism of the young, I believed that the Church of England would surely be ordaining women by the time I was ready.

It wasn't. In 1975, the year I began to study theology at university, the General Synod of the Church of England threw out a motion which would have opened the way for women's ordination. Disillusioned, I decided to go as far as I could — and joined the Movement for the Ordination of Women in the meantime. I received my degree in theology from Durham University, trained for ministry as a deaconess at Ripon College, Cuddesdon (as the first woman seminarian there), and was ordained to the diaconate in 1981 with my husband, David Howells. Paradoxically, after the service he emerged as a deacon in holy orders; I was a deaconess, but still deemed to be a laywoman.

When David was automatically ordained priest one year later, I found it very difficult to bear the church's rejection of me — for rejection was implicit. It was a crisis point for us. We decided to complete our curacy and then move to a country elsewhere in the Anglican Communion where I could realistically test and perhaps fulfil my vocation to the priesthood. We moved to Canada in 1984 and by crossing the Atlantic I became a deacon at once. My ordination as a deaconess was recognized for what it was, instead of being treated with a double standard. In 1985

I was ordained priest in Montreal.

From 1986 to 1990 we shared the position of rector in Kapuskasing, in northern Ontario. With three small children by then, we became practitioners of the art of juggling as we shared both our domestic and our parochial roles.

It was demanding work, with the daily joys and frustrations any parish priest experiences, coupled with those any working parent knows. But I valued immensely the freedom simply to be able to get on with my job. My ordination was not an issue. My energies were not being diffused in battling and bitterness, as they had been in England. And it was an enormous privilege to work with ordained women of other denominations from time to time, knowing that we were evolving a way for women to be God-bearers within the structures of the church; structures which in the past had so often been stultifying and God-denying.

In 1990 David and I moved again, this time out of parochial ministry and into chaplaincy at the University of Guelph. It was a deliberate step sideways, away from the buildings, traditions, congregation, activities, and expectations of a parish, and into a role defined as ecumenical, pastoral, educative, but otherwise gloriously free from constraints.

In parish ministry I had begun to realize what an enormous distance still lies between traditional Christianity as practised by its faithful adherents, and the vision of Christianity and the church being developed by Christian feminists. There were times when I felt that as a woman in what had been a man's role, I was being gently co-opted into a system which was essentially unchanged and which would absorb my own insights and spirituality as a lake engulfs a drop of water. Ordaining women is one thing: allowing women to change patterns of thought, ways of worshipping, styles of leadership, is another.

The parish was not the right place for me to be liturgically radical! Neither was it eager to study issues such as feminist spirituality, ecological theology, psychotherapeutic theory — issues which were increasingly calling me. I was disappointed, but accepted that I could not make the parish in my own image. To explore those regions for myself I had to move on again. And so to university chaplaincy.

My journey so far has been swift. I cannot forget the women in England who had no such escape route. As the situation there slowly and traumatically unfolds, the umbilical cord which still connects me transmits the pain. I feel almost guilty for my good fortune.

But one thing which I have learned is not to be apologetic about who I am. Timidity, self-doubt, uncertainty, exaggerated feelings of guilt — these are the classic sins of women. We do not characteristically commit the sin of pride so frequently highlighted by male theologians and spiritual writers. I am learning to be bold, to dare, to think beyond my immediate boundaries. Life is too short to be wasted in sterile arguments or cautious hesitancy. There is simply too much to be done.

The thought of one day returning to England as a priest is always at the back of my mind. But for now I am content to live as a Canadian. We have a card by our door which reads, "Bloom where God plants you." It reminds me that our permanent roots are in God, however much the soil around us shifts.

Erica Murray

S t. Luke's, Regina, on the Saskatchewan prairies, is a long way from South Africa where I was born and where I worked full time in the church from 1968 to 1984. I have been incumbent here since October 1988.

"Come and work in the parish of Empangeni (Zululand) and see if you can face working in the church!" the Revd Don Griswold said to me in 1965. That was the beginning! After graduate studies in Adult Education and Theology in Boston, I returned to South Africa where I held educational positions in Durban, Cape Town, Umtata (Theological College), and finally in Kimberley where I was Director of Training for Ministries (lay and clergy). Over the years, the question of ordination did not raise its head for me personally. It was not possible for women to be ordained, though I served on one of the many commissions on the subject. The positions I held *could* have been impossible. "All the women who worked here before had nervous breakdowns," in Cape Town, and, in Umtata, "the clergy will never accept a woman teaching them!" In reality, they were possible. However, the bishop would not let me preach at the eucharist at the Theological College, even though I was responsible for spiritual direction for some of the students. In Kimberley, I was an examining chaplain which did not endear me to some clergy — they were happy for me to do the work but didn't like me having the title!

The Church of the Province of South Africa finally decided to allow women to be ordained to the diaconate. The only difference that would have made to my ministry was a title which I did not want. However my husband, at that time, suggested that I include ordination to the priesthood as one of the possibilities when seeking God's will about my future. To my surprise, it seemed that God clearly wanted me to be ordained. Testing God's will meant saying No to the other possibilities and exploring Canada or the USA where women could be ordained. In the meantime, I taught high school so that we could save some money. As several possibilities overseas fell through, we began to think that ordination could not be God's will. One morning, out of the blue, I was invited to the diocese of Central Newfoundland for a three-week period as consultant and trainer. We decided that, if it was God opening a door, I had to accept. I went, armed with references for both of us. Bishop Mark Genge was amazingly understanding but was concerned that there be a "love for the people." After examining my qualifications, the bishop offered us the parish of Bay L'Argent on the understanding that I do some "in-depth" study of the Reformation and Anglican theology.

We arrived in Bay L'Argent in July 1985 for a team ministry in the nine-congregation parish. I was ordained deacon in November 1985, and priested in April 1986, at Harbour Mills. Prior to ordination to the priesthood, I went to New York City for an eight-day directed retreat during which God took away my doubts about being a priest.

In June 1987, I was left alone. My husband had a nervous breakdown and went to Toronto for a new life in journalism, his first love. Fortunately, Newfoundlanders understand "nerves" in a way that no other culture does, so his departure was accepted. I had to cope with the separation and finally a divorce.

Ministering alone in a nine-point parish was quite an experience. I drove 3000 kilometres a month. Life was much easier when I purchased a 4-wheel drive car. The only problem then was that I could get to the places, but the weather was too bad for the people to come out! In Newfoundland, I discovered that the priest was often feared as the bearer of bad news. I learned to preface my calls with, "I've just come to visit — it is not bad news!" Visiting in Newfoundland was easy as people were generally home. In Regina, visiting is complicated by both parents working and children being involved in many activities.

My most "fun" wedding was across the Bay. They came for

me in a "flat" (boat with motor) and brought me back after the ceremony. There were no cars in the community, so we could watch the bridal party leaving their homes and walking to the church. My very first funeral was a matter of "flying by the seat of my pants." I had never been to an Anglican gravesite before. In Newfoundland, I was often expected to read the will after the funeral. My most moving funeral was one of two Anglicans in a Roman Catholic community. We held the eucharist in the Roman Catholic church, then I went with the coffin in a boat leading all the other boats to the place of burial.

I haven't had to face too much prejudice as a priest. In Newfoundland, the fact that the bishop had ordained me was sufficient, though many were worried about me driving in bad weather. In the city, people can choose another parish. One woman was going to leave the parish but came one day and fell in love with my dog. Her fears about women priests were allayed.

For most of the time, being ordained has been a "wilderness" experience for me. Most of my crutches and securities were gone — new country, being alone and adjusting to being single, not being known in the Canadian church and therefore not being respected. Has it all been worth it? Sometimes I have wondered. But I *am* sure that I am doing God's will in being ordained. Ministering as a priest is a privilege. Weekly sermon preparation forces one to read, administering the sacraments is still special, and being a means of God's grace has made me more dependent on God.

"For all that has been, thanks,
For all that will be, yes." (Dag Hammarskjold)

Elizabeth McWhae

God has an uncanny way of surprising people and turning their lives upside down. One minute I am an atheistic medical student living in Adelaide, South Australia, and the next I am a born again, fundamentalist Baptist verging on the charismatic (excuse the labels but it gives you some sort of mental picture of what I was like), still living in Adelaide, and studying medicine. So how, you may wonder, did I end up in a small country town on the Saskatchewan prairies working as an Anglican parish priest?

The story goes like this. I finished my medical training in Adelaide. Like the calls of all good Christian ladies to ministry, everybody was convinced that my call was to be a medical missionary. I myself was not fully convinced of the medical part of this call, but did see myself as being called to some form of ministry. So I went to India to see what being a medical missionary was like. I enjoyed my time tremendously and confirmed what I had felt all along: that I did not wish to become a medical missionary, but I did want to be involved in pastoral ministry.

Once back in Australia I wrestled with what to do. It seemed as if I was in a bind. The more medical work that I did, the more I wanted to be doing something else. But every time I mentioned this to someone they would say that I was a good doctor and why would I want to give it up. Eventually I decided that I would start studying theology and do medical work half-time. I still was not sure what God was calling me to, but knew that I needed some training in theology and pastoral care.

So I embarked upon my studies, and what a journey that was. I discovered that my fundamentalist understanding of faith needed some reworking and in the process somehow ended up

in the Anglican church. From there I began studying at St. Bar-
nabas' Theological College in Adelaide and continued working
in general practice. Life was very hectic, but enjoyable. I still did
not see where all this was leading me.

I was quite adamant that I did not wish to be ordained, largely
because, in retrospect, I was afraid of the reaction people would
have. The issue of the ordination of women was a hot one and
I did not wish to end up being seen as ''one of those crazy
feminists who want to be ordained.'' As events progressed it
became clear to me that the gifts that God had given me could
be well used in ordained ministry. But, I did not want to open
this Pandora's box. Eventually God decided to open it for me.
It first came in the form of a course I took in Feminist Theology
which made me confront some issues that I needed to resolve
about women in the church. Then, through a series of incidents,
it became increasingly clear that God was trying to say something
to me about the direction of my life. I began to share what was
going on inside of me with five people who knew me well and
were themselves ordained ministers. Every one of them said that
they felt I had a calling to ordained ministry and the least I could
do was put this to the test. And so I did. I was accepted as a
candidate for ordination in the diocese of Adelaide. I had one
remaining year of study to complete a Bachelor of Theology and
Diploma in Pastoral Studies, which I completed, while still doing
some medical work.

During this year I was becoming increasingly frustrated by
the attitude towards women who believed they were called to
ordained ministry. Even though there were some positive steps
forward, the deep-seated resentment and so-called threat one
posed to those who were opposed to the ordination of women
made me sceptical of just what would happen when women were
ordained to the priesthood in Australia. I felt ambivalent about
what I was letting myself in for. On the one hand I felt tremendous support from MOW and others in the church who were in
favour of the ordination of women; on the other hand I knew
how difficult it was to keep on ministering to people who felt
that you were deceived, misguided, and leading the church astray.

I had been wondering what would happen next when the Appellate Tribunal decided to put the issue of women's ordination on hold yet again. This decision catalysed my thinking and I decided that I would consider looking further afield. My parents and brother and sister had been living in Canada for many years and I came to Canada every two years to visit them. In December 1989 I came for Christmas and while in Canada decided to see if I could meet with several bishops in the Anglican church. This was arranged and I was overcome by the understanding that various bishops showed towards the situation in Australia for women seeking ordination. While I was in Canada various other bishops wrote to me. The outcome of this was a meeting with the bishop of Qu'Appelle before my trip back to Australia and the distinct feeling that I would be returning to Canada.

I returned to Saskatchewan in early August 1990 and was ordained to the diaconate on 14 September 1990 and to the priesthood on 8 December 1990. I am in the parish of Whitesand, a six-point country parish, discovering what it is like to be a parish priest. So far, the experience has been well worth the trials and tribulations I encountered on the journey to this point.

Jeannette A. Stigger

I was closing the door of a little church in the less well-off district of Westcliff-on-Sea in Essex, England, where I worked as a parish worker, when a woman with a small baby arrived. "I've brought him to be baptized," she announced. I explained that the priest-in-charge was away for two weeks; I asked if she would come back then. She looked me up and down and then said, "Well, what's wrong with you?" I told her I was only a parish worker: I couldn't do baptisms. I could have told her that I only visited, and led prayers, I only led the Sunday School, I only prepared youth and adults for confirmation, I only prayed with the dying, spoke to groups and — occasionally — preached. . . . But she wanted a simple answer to her question. I don't think I convinced her.

It wasn't till one missionary term, one marriage, three children and one culture-shock later, that I heard myself saying to a group at a summer conference that I was only a housewife and mother. The people in the group picked it up immediately and challenged me: how dare I say "only"?? For me this was the beginning of a realization that I'd bought into a second-class concept of women's place in society and church. With this growing awareness I began to find an answer to the question posed by the woman with the baby and to see that God's power could be mediated through an ordained woman. I needed a lot of convincing: there were "yes, but's." I had first to accept the concept. Later came the personal challenge. God didn't take No for an answer.

Because I was such a reluctant convert myself, I trust that God can work through me to reach others. In my parish now there is a huge senior high-rise and in this place there have been some delightful surprises. There is a newly-confirmed, 87-year-old man who is convinced that women make better priests than men. There have been many seniors whose initial reluctance to accept my ministry gradually wore away. Often those with little prior experience of the church are the most accepting; some are assisted by one 92-year-old protagonist who assures all new-comers that "God's servant in this place is a woman."

My experience in this "blue-collar" parish has been that the real struggle in my ministry here is not with the seniors, nor with the youth or the young adults, but with those who are in mid-life. As I read it, for them so much has changed, so many of the old norms are now questioned that my very presence threatens one more norm — that of male leadership. A friendly bystander commented recently that, under pressure, methods learned in the sandbox come quickly to the fore. There are days when I wonder whether blue-collar ministry is not one of the hardest places for a woman to be, because the traditions are so entrenched and unquestioning there; and I wonder how many of us are in those places. Those are the days when I return quickly to the places of encouragement: to a supportive clericus and to women in similar positions; in a large city these places are accessible.

One of the positive trends that I see in this diocese is an increasing ability on the part of the clergy to recognize the need for and to seek support. I think this growth in networking is one of women's gifts to ministry. One lady in my parish commented, "Jeannette has got us working together; we never did that before." I think the sense of "working together" is increasingly true of clericus and diocese. However, I have to admit that it took me a year or two before I could let go of the need to prove myself, and allow both my strengths and weaknesses, and to contribute in my own way.

It is no longer extraordinary to have women incumbents here; there is good support from diocesan structures; clergy maternity benefits were recommended from our synod. But some of the old chauvinistic reflexes and attitudes die hard; it requires a constant reminder that we are assisting in the creation of a new, redeemed community in which the wholeness of men's and women's ministry can be expressed. As I read the daily newspaper I know that vision is needed.

In my seminary days, when, as a mature student, I was struggling to get back into study, while keeping the family together and still keeping my hand in at my local parish, one particular reflection of a friend was what kept me going. She said, "You have no idea what that means for us (she meant the women of the parish) to have you assisting at the altar." At that point I was still adjusting to the new perspective! But her words stayed with me. Some time later a very reserved young man with an English background came to me one morning after the service and said that for him there was an experience of the Holy Spirit through this woman's ministry that was totally unexpected. A new understanding had opened up for him, and a fresh affirmation was given to me. Thanks be to God.

*

The Religious Orders

For centuries, women have responded to the vocation to the religious life. Religious orders for women began in the fourth century, early in the life of the church. In these communities, women were able to pray and study, to teach and heal, to assume leadership roles, and to influence the life of the church. Many of the influential women in the early centuries were members of religious orders. St. Hilda (614–680), for example, was the abbess of Whitby and ruled over a double monastery with a house for men as well as a house for women. As abbess, Hilda not only governed the day-to-day life of the members of her community but was also an educator and trained many of the leading churchmen of the day. The religious houses were centres of education, both theological and secular. Hilda took part in the Synod of Whitby (664), an early example of women's involvement in the government of the church.

During the Reformation, monasteries were dissolved and monks and nuns were forced to return to the ordinary life of society. In the nineteenth century, the monastic movement was re-established in the Church of England as a result of the influence of the Oxford Movement, a movement aimed at restoring catholic traditions to the church. Women's orders were the first to be established. In 1841, Pusey received the vows of Marian Rebecca Hughes who, in 1849, founded the Convent of the Holy and Undivided Trinity in Oxford. Many communities for women were founded in the 1840s and 1850s. These were active communities, combining the monastic life of prayer with service to the wider community. The first contemplative order in the Church of England was the Sisters of the Love of God, founded at Fair Acres, Oxford, in 1907. Men's communities developed more slowly, from the 1860s on. The religious communities have played a most important role in the life of the church. They have been houses of prayer and spiritual direction, and have given themselves to the service of others through teaching, nursing, social work, and the work of mission in other countries.

Today Anglican religious communities of women are centres of lively worship and thought, and make a significant contribution to the whole church. In Canada, two orders for women were founded in the last century. The Community of the Sisters of the Church was founded in England in 1870 and a Canadian house was established in 1890. For many years, the sisters ran a girls' school, located first in Toronto and then in Oakville. The convent in Oakville has a ministry of retreats and spiritual direction. The Sisters of St. John the Divine originated in Canada, founded by Hannah Grier Coombe in Toronto in 1884. The sisters operate a rehabilitation hospital, a care facility for senior citizens, and offer retreats and spiritual direction at the convent in Willowdale and the Priory in Edmonton. The Worker Sisters of the Holy Spirit are a more recent foundation. This is an international community for lay sisters, lay workers, and clergy. Members follow a common rule but do not live in community. Their focus is on mission and ministry in the world. For many years, the Sisters of St. Margaret, an American order, worked in Montreal.

Two of Canada's women priests are members of religious orders, and one story is told here. Because their religious life is lived in community, their decision to seek ordination was one in which the whole community was involved. This change in the traditional practice of ordination was not an easy one. It took time to reach the agreement of the community. But the presence of women religious among the ordained brings to us the gifts, not just of themselves, but of their community life and provides us with a visible link with some of the early women educators of our church, such as St Hilda.

Rosemary Anne, S.S.J.D.

I was fifteen when I knew that, had I been a boy, I would seek ordination to the priesthood. I also knew that, being a girl, I could not follow such a calling.

At fifteen, I was the eldest of five children, and, when I was sixteen, child number six was born. Those were the years of the Great Depression and times were hard. Nevertheless I wrote to the bishop of Brandon to ask what service I could offer within the Anglican church. I did not, of course, mention the priesthood, believing this had been a mistaken idea of my own. The bishop, in his reply, suggested training for the order of deaconesses, but added that I was much too young. He went on to say that I should write anyway and enquire. I did so and received information, and the suggestion that I continue my education and apply in a few years' time. Eventually I was offered a Leonard Foundation scholarship and, with this help, I began training. After three years of study, I began parish work under the Downtown Churchworkers' Association in Toronto. I served in this work for seven years, during which time I was ordered deaconess at St. James' Cathedral.

Meanwhile, I had met and become friends with some of the Sisters of St. John the Divine. I became an Associate and, not long after, was admitted to the novitiate. I was a senior member of the order when the opportunity for ordination was finally offered. First I was accepted by the bishop and then, at a special chapter meeting, the Sisters gave their consent. I was ordained to the priesthood on the Feast of St. Hilda, 18 November 1977, at St. Matthias Church, Toronto. It was a joyful occasion, only slightly marred by the public objection of an old friend who could not let the event go unchallenged. One small, but happy note was that St. Matthias was the parish in which the S.S.J.D. had begun its life ninety-three years earlier.

I have been a priest for fifteen years now and have never had a single moment's regret, or once doubted the rightness of my calling. Since I was the first woman member of a religious order to become a priest in Canada, there was some publicity attached to the occasion, which I am glad to say soon subsided. At Edmonton once again I continue, I hope, to fulfil a ministry both as priest and religious. I feel truly blessed by God and am deeply and joyfully grateful.

*

The Diaconate

In Canada, women were ordained as deacons in 1971, and those women who had been ordered deaconess in previous years were accepted as being within the diaconate. Most deacons were ordained priest when that became possible. However, some women, as do some men, feel a call to the permanent diaconate, to a ministry of service which is particularly characteristic of that order of ministry. Here is a woman deacon's story.

Maylanne Whittall

My story is about my decision to be ordained to the diaconate and not the priesthood, and where that has led me. For the last six years, I have been part of a two-person staff team with a church-based network that builds supportive links among church and community activists responding to urban poverty, particularly among single people of low income.

My journey toward ordination was not smooth. After graduating from university, I earned a teaching certificate and a diploma in theology in England. When I returned to Canada, I was hired for two part-time jobs, as director of Christian Education in a parish church, and teacher of religious education in a girls' school. At the time, education was the only kind of church work available to women.

My two years as director of Christian Education were very unhappy. I had understood I was to be part of a clergy team, but instead felt consigned to the care of children without regard for the value of that ministry. When I arrived, I was given an office in the church basement and introduced to the Christian Education committee. I met other parishioners as their children registered for Church School. I had to find my own apartment and used public transportation to travel between my two jobs. The sum of the two part-time salaries I received was only just enough to live on.

When the associate priest arrived four months later, I was painfully aware of the difference in his reception. He was greeted in a celebration of new ministry at the main service, he was invited to people's homes, his name was added to the Sunday intercession list. Housing and car allowance were included in his stipend. He and the rector were given an annual merit increase, while other parish employees, including myself, were given a smaller cost-of-living increase.

When the rector did not invite me to a big party he hosted in the rectory, it made me realize that I was seen to hold a lower social status. This was reinforced at the parish's centennial celebration, when clergy and other dignitaries were vested and included in procession, while my place was downstairs with the children, out of sight and out of people's way.

I experienced a profound sense of injustice, certainly against myself, but also against the children and support staff, the "little ones" of the parish. I resigned from my position there, returned to theological college for a full degree in theology, and struggled to make sense of what had happened.

When the ordination of women to the priesthood was about to become a reality, I felt very ambivalent about becoming part of a system of clericalism in which I had felt so exploited. I felt my choice was either to become a priest and model it in a different way, or to find another avenue altogether for expressing the bond I felt with others who had experienced exploitation or injustice.

Over time, the latter became the route that I followed. I completed a Master of Divinity, was married, and took a part-time teaching position in another girls' school. My husband was opposed to the ordination of women to the priesthood, and for a year before we were married, we more than once thought of calling the whole thing off. In the end, we decided to entrust this conflict, and our relationship, to the Holy Spirit. Since then, he has become a strong advocate of women in the priesthood, and I have found a different model for church leadership in the diaconate — one which is a more authentic expression of my own story and place in the world.

After being ordained as a deacon, and after seven years of teaching in private girls' schools, I became interim deacon-in-charge of an inner city parish and co-ordinator of an ecumenical community ministry. I began to learn about the conditions and hear the stories of people who were poor, homeless, hungry; people who had been discharged from psychiatric hospitals; women who were abused and beaten; people of colour and of different ethnic backgrounds who did not fit into the culture of the Anglican church. I became increasingly aware of a disparity between what I understood to be the values of the gospel and the goals of the institutional church — its financial priorities, its method of intervention in the decisions of the local congregation, its apparent insensitivity to the concerns of the community.

This renewed struggle led me once again to resign from my job. But this time I was linked up with a network of people who were committed to work towards social justice. Some were based in church-related services and missions and had been strongly influenced by the Canadian Urban Training Project. Others were working in women's shelters or social service agencies and had been shaped by feminist values, and many by their own experience as gays and lesbians.

I was hired to co-staff the national Urban Core Support Network, and the Single Displaced Persons Project in Toronto. This powerful network of people has helped me to develop a clear analysis and theology, to acknowledge what is wrong and unjust in society and the church, and to work towards the transformation of these systems with others who share similar values, experiences, and vision.

Being a deacon has given liturgical and spiritual identity to this work. It has helped me to re-value servant ministry when it is offered in partnership with people whose knowledge of poverty and injustice is a source of unexpected gifts and strength. It has allowed me to take a constructive and prophetic role in the church, while remaining connected with the wider human community in all its vulnerability and diversity.

I still find it difficult to relate to an institutional church that is dominated by patriarchal values; that refers to the people of God as "men" and "brothers," to Christ as "King" and to God as "Father Almighty"; that has no consistent ethic or justice; that has difficulty seeing beyond its own boundaries. Yet the church has also been for me a community that gives life and meaning through the gospel, that listens when others don't, that draws together people with gifts of leadership, integrity, and spirit.

I cling to the hope that the church will be transformed into a resurrection community, and am grateful to God and to my sisters and brothers in Christ for nourishing this hope and giving me hints of what is possible here and now.

*

The Clergy Couple

As more women were ordained, some candidates for ordination were clergy wives. Other women and men met their spouses while both were training for the ordained ministry. Some women priests met their priest husbands while both were involved in pastoral ministry. So there are now in Canada a number of clergy couples. The presence of these couples in a diocese has led to new understandings and models of team ministry. It has also raised questions about financial allowances and benefits, housing, parental leave, joint placement. There are very few opportunities in the church for two full-time positions in the same location. How are clergy couples, bishops, and search committees exploring these issues? In the summer of 1993 a conference for clergy couples in the Province of Rupert's Land was held to address the particular concerns of this group.

J. Dianne Tomalin

In some ways I feel the perspective from five years of priesthood is rather short for me to be critically introspective of my ministry. But in others, because of numerous and varied interim positions, together with my work in partnership with my twenty-three years ordained husband, I suspect I have some experiences and thoughts that might be helpful to me and to others.

My ministry itself goes back much further than ordination; than theological college; than the calling to ordained ministry. Its beginning is fogged somewhere in the past of thirty-some years of living before accepting God's call to the specific ministry of the ordained. From Sunday School attendance, to motherhood, to Sunday School teaching, God indeed encouraged, pushed, and matured a rather immature (person and) faith.

With a mother's commitment to Sunday School teaching came my ongoing relationship with the woman I continue to call my Mother in God, the Revd Ruth Taylor. When I first met Ruth, she was the wife of my parish priest, but more importantly, she was his partner in ministry and mission work. Ruth, theologically trained some thirty years before women's ordination, later became the second woman to be ordained in my diocese of Qu'Appelle.

But it was long before her ordination that Ruth, by example and action, encouraged and nourished my participation in the ministry of God. Over the years as a laywoman, Ruth taught, guided, and loved not only me, but many, many others. She involved us in Bible studies, liturgical ministries, ecumenical prayer groups, her teaching missions, and of course Sunday School teaching.

A Spirit-led person, Ruth constantly shared ministry responsibilities with us, trusting God and us to carry out those responsibilities. My favorite "Ruthism" is, "When you are scared or worried that you can't fulfil your ministry commitments, remind God, 'You got me into this, now you get me out!'" Indeed, I have reminded God of this point many a time since first hearing that gem!

As Ruth moved from lay to ordained ministry I experienced the differences in the two ministries. And it was again Ruth's example, together with encouragement from countless others, not least that of my bishop, the Most Revd Michael Peers, that I finally accepted the call to ordination.

In retrospect I can say that Ruth was, and continues to be, both my model and my mentor. And it is Ruth and her husband the Revd Herb Taylor, who have also been the successful working model of clergy couples for my husband, Patrick, and me to follow.

Since my ordination, Patrick and I have shared a parish ministry, with Patrick designated rector and myself part-time assistant (both paid!). While I realize that not all personalities are able to work together, my husband and I both recognize and accept the value of our own and one another's gifts and abilities. Our gifts, abilities, and personalities, complement one another. Indeed, we often find that our combined ministry more than equals the sum of two individuals! We also find that as we pray and minister together we are able to understand and support one another far better than if we were working independently.

We share Sunday liturgical and preaching duties. As a couple we often counsel, teach, and prepare people for baptism, confirmation, and marriage. At other times we do these things as individuals. As individuals we are both involved in various diocesan roles. Much of our pastoral ministry is done as individuals, but we often find it too is enriched when we work together.

We share duties at weddings and funerals. After many weddings (and even one funeral!) people, including those of other denominations, have made a point of telling us how special they found the service because it was shared by a husband and wife. While no one has ever been able to articulate their reasons theologically, I believe that subconsciously they experience the wholeness of the image of God — In His image He created them, male and female He created them.

Our parish continually affirms the effectiveness of our shared ministries and is working toward increasing my part-time position so that I can spend more time in the parish. Until that time I shall probably continue doing interim ministry as my bishop has need of me.

Actually, the stress I sometimes suffer in ministry can be attributed more to the fragmentation I feel when I am involved in ministry in two or three different communities at the same time, rather than to the team ministry I share with my husband. We find working together as a married, ordained couple, more rewarding and enriching than if we were either two unmarried, ordained people or husband and wife working in different professions. We look forward to continuing in shared ministry and to the time when we might share a joint appointment as co-rectors of a parish.

Ruth Taylor

I believe in miracles. My journey to ordination is one of them. From day one, I had a love-hate relationship with the church. It was nice being in church; I listened eagerly to the scripture and sang the hymns lustily if squeakily, the pitch always too high for comfort. But the foreign language of the long-winded prayers and the incomprehensible sermons bored me to tears. I hated wearing a hat and gloves, hated the punishing discomfort of the pews, but most of all I hated Sunday School, the noise and lack of discipline, being constantly talked down to by perfumed and kindly, but quite ineffectual, well-meaning souls. At age eleven I was confirmed, having readily memorized the catechism without understanding it at all, not because I was ready but because my best friend was being confirmed. I found other churches equally uninspiring. Inside me was a hunger that I couldn't define. The only thing that spoke to me was scripture which I read daily and diligently, thanks to my mother's encouragement. My frustration grew. I was haunted by the conviction that the church ought to be a lot of things to me that it obviously wasn't. Never did it meet my particular needs nor did it care about me as a person. Still I was impelled to persevere with it.

Meanwhile I carried in my heart a passage of scripture heard as a five-year-old — Jesus' command to Peter, "Feed my lambs." The words revolved frequently in my mind. Not until years later did I recognize it as my initial call to priesthood. In my late teens, I made serious enquiries about training as a deaconess, but there was little encouragement. Then came the war, service in the armed forces, marriage to a soldier who had aspirations to the priesthood, and the trauma of post-war adjustments. In 1947, we found ourselves in charge of the Indian residential school on James Bay with 2 1/3 children of our own, besides the hundred in our care. It was a make-or-break experience. By the grace of God, we emerged with our faith in God intact but my faith in the church even more badly shaken.

My husband was ordained deacon in June 1949. Six months later, we were catapulted into parish life with no training, no orientation, no money, no furniture, a suitcase full of second-hand clothing, two pre-schoolers, and a retarded baby. Welcome to the world of clergy wives, Ruth. Unpaid curate. One-woman Altar Guild. Poverty. Impossible expectations on all sides. Loneliness. A non-person — the rector's wife. Perpetual fatigue. No friendly or sympathetic ear. Smiling on the outside, silently weeping on the inside. The church had done it again — stolen my husband's time, attention, and affection. A deep abiding anger was born in me, an anger that grew, nourished by insensitivity, injustice, and frustration. The love-hate relationship expanded to include my husband, his work, and the church. I couldn't live with, or without, any of them. Eighteen months in a downtown parish in southern Ontario extended my education. Being a poor curate's wife is even worse than being the rector's wife! May God bless them all!

Back to Moosonee, and at last some sunshine — the initiation of a healing ministry in our large and booming parish. Suddenly God became real and personal to me. Prayer became a viable, enjoyable, and profitable expenditure of energy. I began to feel like a person again as people asked me for prayer. A vision took shape in my mind of what the church ought to be, and could be. I enrolled in a theology course through an Ontario college, gobbling it up like a starved person. Receiving the certificate in 1963 was a personal triumph but short-lived for there I was, all dressed up with nowhere to go! There was no hope of using the degree.

The brightest ray of sunshine came with my appointment as editor of *The Living Message*. Here, on the national board of the Women's Auxiliary, were women like myself with the same love-hate relationship with the church. We shared an urgent call to serve God in the church but were sidetracked into ''auxiliary'' status by closed doors everywhere. We found satisfaction in our accomplishments but felt both used and abused by the institution. They wanted our money, would have foundered completely in many areas without it, but they didn't want us. Here for the first time I found real fellowship and sympathetic understanding, a gift from God when parish life was unbearable. Women were not allowed on vestries, in synod, or in any decision-making position, but were urged to raise money, train the children, and keep the brass shining.

Then General Synod began to consider the ordination of women. Many clergymen, including my husband, vowed to leave the Anglican church if it happened. The idea of women as clergy was dangerous, subversive, and not to be taken seriously. Women in later years have not known the agony of being so totally rejected. It looked as if my deepest desire would never be fulfilled. The editorial page of *The Living Message* was a place to vent my wrath, and there were many occasions for public speaking.

The early seventies saw the charismatic renewal. I found at last the inner healing I so badly needed. My gifts were strengthened and put to use as people came to me for prayer and counsel. The work was so rewarding and exciting that I accepted this ministry as the fulfilment of my calling. But it wasn't. A prophecy at a prayer meeting clearly designated me as a priest. Three different people within a month asked me the same question, ''Ruth, when are you going to be ordained?'' So tentatively I made my first approach to ordination, only to find that all the barriers had vanished. Within two months of the prophecy, I was accepted for ordination. On 21 May 1978, our thirty-fifth wedding anniversary, I was ordained deacon at St. John's, Moose Jaw. At that moment my anger disappeared, never to return. But it was replaced by a kind of sadness for the church.

Priesting followed in November 1979. At the end of the ceremony, I thought that this was nothing new at all. I had always been a priest from the moment God called me to feed his sheep. From that day, joy and peace have never ceased to flow and my heart is filled with gratitude as the journey continues. Yes, miracles do happen!

Aloha L. Smith

I am working in the Anglican diocese of Montreal in Quebec, having been ordained deacon in October of 1988 and priest in May of 1989. My first assignment was as a parish assistant priest and as the Protestant Spiritual Animator in a public, English-language high school.

As a priest, my pastoral and liturgical duties were similar to those of the rector. He reserved the right to make administrative decisions, but in the small parish situation in a non-suburban, town environment, we worked as a team.

As chaplain in a school of 1000 students (grades 7-11), I acted as a resource person to classroom teachers of Moral and Religious Education, and as community liaison and social advocate, taking students on field trips to broaden the scope of the issues they study, and to make the ethical and moral responsibility of citizen to community visible within the school microcosm.

Both this school and the other one I was assigned to following my curacy in the parish had chapels built into them as an accommodation to the English Catholic students drawn into the reorganized school district. In other words, for a little more than two decades, these communities on the South Shore of the St Lawrence were more concerned about the impact of the English exodus and French language laws than they were about traditional Roman Catholic and Protestant schism on the topic of public school religious education.

So, the Roman Catholic chaplain and I worked very hard to make the chapel area available as a "neutral zone" for counselling and recreation during breaks. It was also a place to hold celebrations marking and participating in the cycle of the Christian year. Needless to say, this use of the resources of Christianity to a secularized and very needy population was personally very gratifying and fulfilling as a call to mission.

During the Mohawk crisis of 1989-90 and the outbreak of the Gulf War, the chapels also became places of peace-making and dialogue, where native students, whites, and blacks, could come together and expect a receptive ear and a hearing heart. We learned what we could from the healing circles employed by the leaders in our neighbouring Kawnawake, and I adapted everything I could from the conflict management movement sweeping the inner-city schools in the U.S. I learned a great deal more during that time than I thought.

Trying to develop a team approach for administration, teachers, parents, students, and support staff, was as overwhelming as it was novel, but I was able to sow some seeds for acknowledging personal investment in the management of conflict in the school setting at that time of great stress, and the fruits of it continue on in the work today. Because after I was called to a parish, the school board not only continued the high school chaplaincy programme, by hiring a male Anglican priest to replace me, but also expanded it to the elementary schools in the district by hiring part-time female laypersons.

Probably my first introduction to these ideas pre-dated the school setting, because a part of my pastoral assignment in my seminary days was as an intern to the Jewish-Christian dialogue of Montreal. I continued as a member of that group for four more years, even organizing the shared worship services when their international colloquium met in Montreal in 1988, and visiting Israel in 1990 on the eve of the Gulf War, as part of a fact-finding mission on peace-making.

I have become increasingly concerned with the dangers of acquiescence to Christian imperialism and lack of sympathy for inter-faith understanding. But, at the same time, I have become even more aware of the genuine and life-transforming power of the love of Christ as we bear it, often in silence, to all those we meet in the world.

I have taken a very long time to get to this place. I am the wife of a clergyman, ordained in 1974 after a probationary period following our divorces and marriage to each other. I had been conscious of a vocation to ordained ministry for fifteen years, but I felt unworthy of ordination and certainly unencouraged by anyone in ecclesiastical authority to pursue it.

With a background in musicology and performance of renaissance music, I taught in Vermont country schools and New Jersey inner-city schools with the growing conviction that arts education was a human right, and most needed by the most disadvantaged. I learned skills in dealing with all age groups from pre-kindergarten to college, and ended up with an incompleted M.Ed. thesis on cognitive development, as my attempt to fulfil the unwritten rule that women have to have a Master's degree in another field before applying for postulancy.

In our parish moves from rural to wealthy suburban to inner city, I acquired ministry skills appropriate to the area, and kept growing spiritually with encounters in the Cursillo movement, scripture study, and spiritual direction. When my husband felt a call to minister in a "renewed" suburban parish near Montreal, my family coped with the Quebec language challenges for our school-age children, and we left the U.S.A. for Canada.

After another year of teaching in a private, Christian school to test my vocation, I entered McGill University to take B.Th. and S.T.M. degrees, and the M.Div. degree from the neighbouring diocesan college in four years of full-time study. I was not supported with hopes for a parish placement or work as part of a clergy couple, which has been Bob's and my mutual vocation and hope.

The first year of seminary, I remained in my husband's parish, filling my usual job as organist and choir master, liturgist, and Christian music educator. In a place not known for music education in English, my work in the church filled a spiritual and artistic gap, unprecedented in my experience. But after starting a handbell choir and undergirding both children's and adult music, drama, and dance participation in church and community, I was assigned as a ministry student in another suburban parish, taking a three-year break from these responsibilities.

All along, we kept in contact with the diocesan leadership

to renew our plea to work together as salaried priests in the same parish. But at that time, the model was too unknown in this area for acceptance. This "top-brass" attitude of pre-formed judgements and apprehension has been a drain on energy and a test of spiritual depth. Through it all, my husband and I have been very conscious of God's love and guidance. Affirmation has always come, often from very unexpected sources, and correction from God has been gentle — encouraging rather than eliminating growth. I have been very conscious that "self-control" and "steadfastness" (II Peter 1:6) are steps to which women clergy are called in our Way of the Cross.

And so my curacy assignment was in a church far from my home, over a disputed bridge, later arrayed with Canadian Army tanks. My daily travel was, for a short time, across a "war zone."

As I have opened this article with that experience, I hope I make it clear that Providence had a strong hand in providing me with a rich, inter-cultural, community and institutional experience I could simply never have gained any other way. And I am truly grateful for it, including the 5,000 km. months my intrepid little Chevette put in to reach my two high schools. Because yes, after my curacy period was up, unlike the other diocesan college students, I was not offered another church. I was told that being a clergy wife, I was hard to place and my two years of travel did not seem to qualify me as an expert on a non-residential priesthood.

However the local ministerial association — French and English Roman Catholic, Pentecostal, Baptist, United, Presbyterian, and Anglican clergy — had other ideas. Monies had actually been set aside, unused, by the Quebec government for some years for the purpose of enabling Protestant high school chaplaincy in Quebec. So the school board in conjunction with the clergy, applied to receive some of them. The application was successful. I left my formal association with the parish church, and began working with the staff of both places, with a combined student population of about 1,700. I became a priest, in effect, for the Quebec government! This all has affirmed my view that God, indeed, has a sense of humour.

Before this call, I was imbued with an individualistic and critical spirit which judged each person and condition. I still battle with the critical spirit, and do not often win, but I have been taught that enduring, pastoring, and making sense of it is my job. Judging it is God's.

During seminary, the few women in the college shared with each other the fears, manipulations, and pressures to which we had been subjected in this setting. None of us had any power. None of us had any wordly base to fall back on, to heal and nurture us if this vocational quest were denied. We found that disinformation about each other was a tool for control, and economic and spiritual insecurity was our greatest threat.

We had almost no time to spend together, and the chapel community was not one where we could publicly offer up prayers for the situation. We needed community prayer, and were supported by the example of a laywoman who had made a list of women students in Canada and prayed for them. In the midst of a mutual crisis at one point, I made a list of psalms from an Order of Saint Helena breviary, and we agreed that, as much as we could with our diverse duties and schedules, we would pray them, separated by distance but united in spirit. That mutual crisis began to pass, and the dark clouds started to lift. One by one, each of us was affirmed in various personal ways. Sometimes we commented that hope was starting to return. We felt stronger.

Some of us did not survive the seminary process, and a great deal of healing is still needed. Those of us who were ordained still need to work out the spiritual "charley-horses" of being continually called into question. All of us are clear on one thing. God loves us deeply and personally, and is calling us into God's service. This assurance is our greatest gift to those we pastor.

I am "mother" and "mom" to my congregation partly because I am being mothered by God at a time when my fathers in God find it difficult to be fatherly. And besides, as a mother of two, I answer to it anyway! It is an interesting footnote for many of us that our college principal published a short article and subsequent letter in 1992 editions of the *Anglican Journal* on the concept of the "motherhood of God" found in

James 1:18. In some ways, the revelation which affirmed our own, was somewhat too late to undo the past. But in other ways, the work many of us have been called to do on the sociology of gender understanding about God's relation to us and our relation to each other is a gift born out of that long struggle to be understood and heard.

After a year of working in my husband's parish as a volunteer honorary assistant, I have been working full time this year as his salaried associate priest. Adjustments in both the diocese and the parish made it possible. We continue to pray and learn together how to make it normal. Through intensive summer work, we have been pursuing Doctorate of Ministry degrees, focussing on the concept of complementarity in gender relationships. One exciting aspect of this is getting to meet other couples in ministry across North America, and hear their stories.

In addition, we have been working on joint Pastoral Counseling certification, meeting in supervisory groups to understand better the dynamics, difficulties, and deep fecundity of what it might mean to Mr. and Mrs. Cleopas and their church on our own road to Emmaus.

Our studies on complementarity in parish ministry, my regular column on Christian Education, "Now, Go!", in our diocesan monthly, and my directorship of *Crossroads*, a diocesan worship service for young people, sponsored by Crosstalk Ministries, keeps me reflecting and continually wondering how we got this way, and how we can get it better.

Twin quotations are a single watchword. Professor Prudence Allen, R.S.M., cites the first one, quoting Heraclitus (5th c., B.C.E.) in her book on the Aristotelian roots of Christian theology. [*The Concept of Woman*, Montreal, 1985, pp. 18, 19]

"Perhaps Nature has a liking for opposites and produces concord out of them and not out of similars, just as for instance she brings male together with female and not with members of the same sex. . . 'would that strife were destroyed from among gods and men' for there would be no harmony without sharps and flats, no living beings without male and

female, which are contraries.''

The other is my loosely-translated version of Colossians 1:17.

''Christ exists before anything else that is, and, in Christ, all things hang together!''

Thank God for it. Alleluia!

*

Introduction to the Story of Lois Wilson

The United Church of Canada has now ordained women to the ministry of word and sacrament for fifty-seven years. Although our churches have different histories and traditions, different theologies of ministry and church government, yet the struggle for ordination and acceptance is remarkably similar to our own. The stories of United Church women, whose struggles for acceptance continued for years after ordination was permitted in principle, remind us that we are all still in the process of pioneering. Our Anglican sacramental view of priesthood is thought by some to be a barrier to the acceptance of the ordination of women. Yet there are clearly other factors at work — the interpretation of scripture, the place of women in Canadian society, the use of power and authority in the church. The story of Lois Wilson, ordained almost thirty years after the first ordination of women in the United Church, reminds us that the full acceptance of the role of women in the life of the church is a very long process.

Lois Wilson

My ordination must be understood in the context of the history of the ordination of women in the United Church of Canada, a 1925 Union of Presbyterians, Methodists, and Congregationalists in Canada, with the further addition of the Evangelical United Brethren in the mid-sixties. One of the uniting churches, the Congregationalists, had ordained women long before that church came to Canada, but no woman came forward in Canada until 1925, when a candidate appeared in the person of Lydia Gruchy. Gruchy had experienced some frustration working as a deaconess for the church in Saskatchewan, because she was barred from administering the sacraments or performing marriages. She always had to call in "a real minister," although she was a theological graduate and had all the responsibilities of a male minister. Her application for ordination to Kamsack Presbytery in 1925, the year of Union, began a process within the church that finally resulted in her ordination in 1936. In pursuing her goal, she thrust the church into what turned out to be a long debate on the merits of ordaining women.

In 1928, the highest court of the United Church, its General Council, declared "there was no bar in religion or reason to the ordination of women to the ministry." But there were plenty of other obstacles, not the least of which were cultural assumptions about the proper role of women, informed by a patriarchal culture that still dominated decision making in Canada. In 1964, two years before I became a candidate, the Toronto newspapers were featuring negative headlines about Margaret Butler, a married woman with a child, who had asked for ordination. Many thought that ordination was meant only for single women and this attitude had persisted.

In 1962 only one recommendation of the Commission on Ordination was adopted by General Council. It declared that ordination would be open only to those women who were unmarried or were widows or who were ''at the time in life when they were no longer required in the home as mothers.'' Female ordination would be contemplated only if a suitable ministry could be arranged which did not interfere ''with the stability of the marriage and their position as wives'' so that they would ''therefore be able to fulfil the vows of ordination.'' My husband, Roy, happened to be at that General Council. He was one of sixty-two out of about four hundred delegates who insisted that their negative votes be recorded, because they saw the resolution as too restrictive for women.

That same year, the congregation of Thunder Bay's First United in northern Ontario, where Roy had been minister since 1960, threw out the suggestion that I might consider ordination as I had received my theological degree in 1950 but had not sought ordination at that time. It was a congregation with extensive pastoral responsibilities, and Roy was called on for many services by folk outside the congregation. Our fourth and youngest child, Bruce, was only two at the time, and I was not ready to seek ordination and give myself ''wholly'' to the ministry. I did, however, become the part-time, paid Pastoral Assistant to the congregation.

The congregation sent out the word across the country that another minister was needed for a staff team in Thunder Bay. After two years of advertising and searching, only two responses were received, and both applicants were considered unacceptable to the congregation. So the wheel came full circle. Would I think again about ordination? I was doing most of the work of a minister anyway. By this time Bruce was four, and I was ready to consider the suggestion.

I had been thinking of scarcely anything else for two years, but was still uncertain. The debate in my own family was far from over as shown by one of my clergyman father's 1964 letters:

At the time you might have been ordained, you were set to

be married, and could not promise to give yourself wholly
to the work of ministry. I doubt very much whether a request
for ordination at that time and under those circumstances
would have been accepted. You knew you could not put yourself at the disposal of the Settlement Committee. (This Committee assigns ministers to their first ordained pastorate, and
that could be anywhere in Canada — my note.)

You are at the place where you could raise quite an issue.
You could propose a new pattern. When a man promises to
give himself wholly to ministry, our Church does not interpret that to mean celibacy. We are quite sold on the idea
that a male minister is not barred because he has wife and
family and is expected to give time to them. But the Church
seems to feel that while these responsibilities do not bar the
man from ordination, they do bar the woman! I can see quite
a battle shaping up.

Almost all the men I consulted (particularly United Church
clergy) counselled me against ordination. With one accord they
told me that I would be much more effective doing volunteer
work as a minister's wife. Rev. J.R. Mutchmor, the Moderator
of the day, offered three reasons against my being ordained? First,
who would "wear the pants" in the family? He thought two
ministers in a family would precipitate marital conflict. Secondly,
who would get the priority use of the car? It never occurred to
him that we might each have a car. Thirdly, he warned that a
husband and wife team could intimidate a congregation and operate as a power bloc. I conceded that the third objection might
be something to watch out for, but if sensitively handled should
not be an insuperable impediment.

Finally, in 1964, the restriction on the ordination of married
women was removed by the General Council. Early in 1965 I
decided to seek ordination. Our children were in nursery and
elementary school, and were already partly in the care of the wider
community. I felt called to ministry and my call had been vali-
dated by the Christian community who already felt free to use
my services frequently.

A key question when considering candidates for ministry was the candidate's availability to give himself or herself "wholly" to ministry. Much hinged on the interpretation of what "wholly" meant. On 3 March 1965, I wrote a letter to Winnipeg Presbytery, indicating that I wished to seek ordination.

> The question is, am I prepared to give myself "wholly" to the work of ministry? When a man is ordained, we recognize that a wife and children are a legitimate part of the life of a minister. Indeed, the manse family is one of the strongest witnesses for the Protestant faith. I feel that I am in a position to give myself as wholly to the ministry as does my husband.
>
> I realize I do not fit any neat category. If the church does grant me ordination, then I would anticipate working out a "team ministry" with my husband here at First Church. We will not, of course, be here for life, but I am certain there will be other opportunities open up across Canada. Indeed, to ordain me might even open up those opportunities.
>
> I find it impossible then, to put myself in the hands of the Settlement Committee if this means sending me to a distant charge. But if I was ordained, we might work out some new pattern for the church and its ministry, perhaps a team ministry being a beginning.

Contrary to my father's prediction, it turned out not to be a battle. The major reason things went so smoothly was that the congregation strongly supported my candidacy with the appropriate courts of the church. I was not perceived as a woman who was demanding her "rights," but as one in whom the local congregation wished to vest responsibility and spiritual leadership. I had been happily practising lay ministry as an adult Christian. All along I had not wanted ordination unless the community of faithful people affirmed "the call."

My final interview took place the afternoon before the evening ordination service at the United Church in Portage la Prairie, Manitoba. Since the interview took place at 2 p.m. and the service was at 8 p.m. I didn't know until a few hours beforehand whether or not I would be included in the service. When it became obvious that it was going to happen, and that protocol demanded all candidates appear in ordination garb, I borrowed a black choir gown from the choir room of the church where we were meeting, hastily hemmed it up so I wouldn't trip, and presented myself for the procession along with four other candidates, all men. My father and Roy joined with church officials in the "laying on of hands." It never occurred to me to include a woman in the ceremony. I was ordained in 1965, on my fifteenth wedding anniversary. It's one of the few times I've seen my husband, Roy, with tears in his eyes. My children greeted my return to Thunder Bay with a crayoned sign, "Welcome Home, Reverend Mother." Since the area we ministered in was called Superior Presbytery, I told my colleagues they could call me Mother Superior.

Since that time, I have been minister in shared pastorates with my husband in Thunder Bay, Hamilton, and Kingston, Ontario. I was elected the first woman as President of the Canadian Council of Churches, and Moderator of my church 1980–82, which is its highest elected office. In 1983 I was elected as one of seven Presidents of the World Council of Churches and wrote of that experience in a memoir, *Turning the World Upside Down.*

What frustrates me still is the obvious surprise with which one is greeted after service with the comment, "That was a very good sermon." I get very tired of having to be constantly alert to the subtle ways in which women clergy are sidelined, ignored, or fawned over. My main learning has been to act in the knowledge that I, too, am made in the image of God, and that acts or attitudes of discrimination and prejudice are the problem of the other person, not mine. I hope that the Spirit will enlighten them soon.